MAKERS
of the
MUSLIM
WORLD

Akbar

For current information and details of other books in the
series, please visit www.oneworld-publications.com

MAKERS
of the
MUSLIM
WORLD

Akbar

ANDRÉ WINK

ONEWORLD
OXFORD

A Oneworld Book

Published by Oneworld Publications 2009

Copyright © André Wink 2009

ISBN 978–1–85168–605–6

Typeset by Jayvee, Trivandrum, India
Printed and bound in India for Imprint Digital

Oneworld Publications
185 Banbury Road
Oxford OX2 7AR
England
www.oneworld-publications.com

Learn more about Oneworld. Join our mailing list to
find out about our latest titles and special offers at:

www.oneworld-publications.com

"Well, I dream'd
That stone by stone I rear'd a sacred fane
A temple, neither Pagod, Mosque, nor Church,
But loftier, simpler, always open-door'd
To every breath from heaven, and Truth and Peace
And Love and Justice came and dwelt therein"

Tennyson, "Akbar's Dream"

CONTENTS

ACKNOWLEDGMENTS

Part of the research for this book was done at the Hebrew University, Jerusalem, in 2005–2006. I am most grateful to the George L. Mosse Program for sponsoring my stay in Israel and to my students and colleagues at the Hebrew University for commenting on some of the ideas elaborated here. Above all, I must thank Professor Patricia Crone for expert editorial advice.

INTRODUCTION

Jalal ad-Din Akbar (1542–1605) was the third ruler of the Mughal dynasty of India. In some important respects, however, he can be regarded as the first. His grandfather, Zahir ad-Din Babur (1483–1530), had invaded the country in 1526 from Kabul, and during the four years that were left to him made the first conquests here. In much of northwestern and northern India power was then in the hands of an immigrant Afghan ("Pathan") clan called the Lodis. Having seized the throne in 1451, these were the last of a long sequence of Muslim kings ruling from Delhi since the beginning of the thirteenth century – the Sultans of Delhi. Babur defeated the Indo-Afghan ruler Ibrahim Lodi (1517–1526) but hardly left a permanent mark in the country. He considered India "a country of few charms," and made his conquests almost by default, after his triple failure to hold Samarqand against more powerful Uzbek rivals. By the time he invaded India, Babur had started to think of Kabul as his home base. At his own request, he was taken back to Kabul after his death in Agra in 1530, to be interred in a modest, uncovered grave in the garden on the western slopes of a mountain that became known as "Babur's Garden."

Babur's son and successor Nasir ad-Din Humayun (1508–1556) – Akbar's father – was forced out of India in 1540 by a short-lived resurgence of Indo-Afghan power under the formidable Sher Shah – not of the Lodi but of the rival Sur clan. Returning to India fifteen years later with an army provided by the Safawid emperor of Persia, Humayun died a year later after a fall in his library.

Most writers on the subject have for these reasons regarded Akbar, succeeding Humayun in 1556, as the real founder of the Mughal empire. For instance, the Venetian physician Niccolao Manucci, who spent the second half of the seventeenth century in the

"Mogor" (as Mughal India was then called in Portuguese), wrote about Akbar: "There is no doubt that this king was the first who brought Hindustan into subjection, and was the most successful in war" (Manucci, I, 147).

Babur and Humayun were important, especially, because through them Akbar traced his pedigree back to the great Turko-Mongol conqueror Timur (Timur-i-Lang or "Tamerlane," d. 1405) by seven generations on his father's side and to the Mongol emperor Chingis Khan (d. 1227) on his mother's side. The remotest origins of the Mughal dynasty of India, in effect, extended back into the legendary past of the horse-riding nomadic tribes of Mongolia – the territory at the eastern end of the vast Eurasian steppe lands. Chingis Khan, having unified the nomadic tribes of Mongolia in 1206 and turned them into his army, conquered China, Central Asia, Khurasan, and then Russia and parts of eastern Europe, thus casting a long shadow as the founder of the Mongol world empire. Genealogical links to Chingis Khan remained the most potent source of legitimacy in the kaleidoscopic mayhem of Turko-Mongol conquest politics of all later times.

Timur was the last great nomadic world conqueror in the Chingisid tradition. He was a genuine nomad of Mongol descent, born in the Chaghatay Khanate near Samarqand, but Muslim by religion and Turkish in speech and culture, and not a Chingisid by genealogical descent. Without a royal pedigree of his own, having started his career as a petty brigand, stealing sheep, he was able to seize the throne of Samarqand in 1369 through sheer military prowess. Timur, however, boosted his position by passing himself off as an amir or "commander" of a Chingisid puppet king and by acquiring the title of *güregen* or royal son-in-law by virtue of his marriage to a Chingisid princess. After his death, the Timurid princes of the fifteenth century, such as Babur, still considered themselves the heirs of all of their illustrious ancestor's conquests between the Mediterranean and Delhi, and from the Volga to the Persian Gulf. In fact, however, they consolidated their power in much smaller dominions on both sides of the Amu Darya. Here – in Samarqand, Bukhara, and Herat – they patronized great architectural projects while living in tents in gardens, not in palaces, in the fashion of nomads, but otherwise turning their backs on the nomadic life of their ancestors.

Babur's grandson Akbar thus had Timurid-Chingisid ancestors who had ruled far-flung nomadic world empires for centuries, but, by the turn of the fifteenth century, were in a state of transition to a more sedentary, post-nomadic condition. The dynasty of the Indian Mughals completed this transition. It was considered primarily Turkish-Timurid in the sixteenth century, since female parentage was insufficient to make it truly Mongol-Chingisid in Central Asia. But because in India there were no claimants to true Chingisid credentials, the name Mughals, which is simply Persian for "Mongols," began to be applied to them fairly soon, and this is how they became known to posterity, even though Babur would not have referred to himself as such and rather would have called himself a Turk and a Timurid.

Akbar's contemporaries seem to have had no doubt that his abilities matched those of his legendary nomadic ancestors. Manucci, in his day still surrounded by people who had personally known the emperor well, wrote that "if any of the Mughal kings inherited the valor and judgment of Timur-i-Lang, it was, without contradiction, the king Akbar" (Manucci, I, 118).

If Akbar inherited any such qualities from Timur or Chingis Khan, he was also fortunate not to have to deal with the vicious sibling and clan rivalry that had always been characteristic of Turko-Mongol politics, and had been the bane of Babur's and Humayun's reigns as well. Among the nomadic Turks and Mongols it was the custom that territory was collectively shared and inherited by all male members of the patriarchal clan. Moreover, since there was extensive intermarriage between clans, their elites became ever more intertwined, further increasing the potential for conflict. The conflict was greatest when nomadic conquerors began to develop more autocratic forms of political control in sedentary areas such as India, where a great deal of wealth (far greater than in nomadic societies) would flow into monarchical hands, corroding the more egalitarian tradition of sharing. Almost all of Babur's political rivals were close relatives. When

Humayun arrived at his first meeting with Shah Tahmasp of Persia and was asked what had led to his defeat by the Afghans, his blunt answer was: "The opposition of my brothers" (MT, I, 569). Akbar, however, faced this problem only to a minor degree. He merely had one half-brother, Mirza Muhammad Hakim, who, being nine years younger, was too young to be a rival when Akbar came to the throne and then, when he grew up, was fitted out with the princely domain of Kabul. From Kabul he could, and did, rally opposition to challenge Akbar's rule on several occasions, but he never became a mortal threat to the latter. Having had a late start, he died young in 1585, and only made history as "the forgotten prince." It was this situation that allowed Akbar to become the real founder of the Mughal empire, as well as its principal architect, and thereby re-establish the fortune of his nomadic ancestors Chingis Khan and Timur — in the sedentary lands beyond the Indus that had mostly eluded them in their own days. Among the Great Mughals (1526–1707) only Akbar's son Jahangir (1605–1628) was blessed with an equal lack of politically dangerous brothers. In Jahangir's case it was because his two brothers and rivals for the throne died in their early thirties from the effects of alcoholism, when Akbar was still on the throne.

1

DIVINE NURSLING OF THE GARDEN OF SOVEREIGNTY

Commensurate with its importance, Akbar's very long reign is well-documented in historical chronicles and other accounts, as well as in memoirs and letters composed by contemporaries from almost all over the world. Among the most important sources of information are Abu-l-Fazl's lengthy works, the *Akbarnama* and *Ain-i-Akbari*, which are invariably sympathetic to him; Badauni's *Muntakhab at-Tawarikh*, which is highly critical of Akbar's religious policies; and the letters sent home from Akbar's court by Jesuit missionaries. Together with the other materials, these sources provide us with a picture of Akbar which is, in Muslim India, without question unprecedented in its historical and biographical detail, even though the introspective depth and frankness of autobiographical writings like that of his grandfather Babur are lacking, and Akbar never wrote anything of his own.

Nevertheless, we know relatively little about Akbar's early life before he came to the throne in 1556, because the chronicles treat it as a subordinate part of Humayun's reign. Of Akbar they say little. As accounts of Humayun's reign from its early stages, the Indo-Muslim chronicles focus their attention on the opposition and "traitorous" conduct of Akbar's three uncles, the Mirzas ("Princes") Kamran, Askari, and Hindal, which contributed so much to Humayun's defeat and ousting by the Afghans. They explain how Kamran was allowed to retain possession of Kabul (a special princely concession because of its association with Babur) and of the Panjab, with its capital of Lahore, and how in 1539 there was an attempt to set Humayun aside for his brother Hindal which almost led to his abdication. They conclude with an account of the two crushing defeats inflicted on Humayun by Sher Shah and the Afghans, at Chausa on June 27, 1539, and at Kanauj on May 17, 1540.

The subsequent flight of Humayun to Sind, and his onward journey to Persia, are generally described by Abu-l-Fazl in euphemistic terms as "the coming of Sher Khan [not 'Sher Shah']," "the departure [*rihla*]," "that unavoidable event," or "that time [when] the imperial army marched to subdue the country of Tatta [Sind]" (AN, I, 55; Ain, 347, note 1). This brings the narrative to Akbar's birth.

AKBAR'S BIRTH

Accompanied by his half-brother Hindal, Humayun moved down the Indus in the hope of collecting an army in Sind and returning to Hindustan via Gujarat, while his two other brothers, Kamran and Askari, withdrew to Kabul together. He allegedly spent two and a half years, from early 1541 to mid-1543, in Sind and Rajasthan, in an unsuccessful attempt to turn his fortune around. It was during this otherwise fruitless interval, when the fugitive Mughal emperor was more than once reduced to destitution, that Akbar was born.

Humayun met the future mother of Akbar, Mariam Makani Hamida Banu Begam, at a party in his brother Mirza Hindal's camp. "Hamida" was a Persian Shi'a Muslim, the daughter of Hindal's tutor Shaykh Ali Akbar. She is said to have been fourteen years of age when, on August 21, 1541, she married (after understandable hesitation) the thirty-three-year-old Humayun. She accompanied Humayun when he left Sind in May 1542 for Rajasthan. At that time Humayun was proposing an alliance with the powerful Raja of Marwar (present-day Jodhpur), Maldeo (Malla Deva), in an attempt to recover Hindustan from Sher Shah, by way of Jaisalmer. Receiving threats and diplomatic overtures from Sher Shah, the Raja changed his mind about the proposed alliance with Humayun. With Hamida now nearly eight months pregnant, Humayun and his small following had to make their way back across two hundred miles of loose sand desert during the hottest time of the year. This was the historic moment when the prospects of Humayun, and the Mughal dynasty as such, reached an all-time low. Horses and camels were dying, the remainder of the royal retinue was melting away, and the emperor had to borrow desperately needed cash from one of his nobles at an exorbitant rate. To make things even worse, the Raja of Jaisalmer ordered the wells to be filled with sand in retaliation for Humayun's men having killed some cows in the region. The party, nonetheless, made its way to the relatively safe surroundings of Umarkot, a village in Sind which the sources describe as a beautiful place with tanks, and the site of a fortress. Humayun left his family and dependants here while he himself joined the local ruler in a campaign against Bhakkar in return for an offer of seven thousand horsemen recruited from the local tribes.

Akbar was born at Umarkot three days after Humayun's departure for Bhakkar, on October 11, 1542, at an astrologically propitious hour. "The unique pearl of the vice-regency of God came forth in his glory," wrote Abu-l-Fazl, "and at his birth at the first opening of his eyes on the visible world, rejoiced the hearts of the wise with a sweet smile" (AN, I, 57, 132). Another contemporary historian, al-Qandahari, has it that the future emperor at the time of his birth "kept his eyes on the stars," as wise men do (TAK, 24). The news of Akbar's auspicious birth was rapidly conveyed to Humayun at his camp in a place called Jun, on the Indus river. Akbar was carried over there in a litter with his mother, together with the entire Umarkot entourage, when he was six months old.

SEPARATED FROM HIS PARENTS

In 1543, Humayun, suffering massive defections at his camp at Jun, tried to make his way to Qandahar. He crossed the Indus on July 11, but found the road cut off by his brothers Kamran and Askari. He was then persuaded by one of his remaining amirs, Bairam Khan, who had ancestral ties to the Persian royal family, to move on to Iran.

For Humayun this was the beginning of another long period of insecurity and hardship. The struggle between Humayun and his brothers would not be decided until ten years later, when it cleared the way for the final Mughal re-conquest of Hindustan. Hindal eventually died in 1551, fighting on Humayun's side. Askari spent a long time in chains before he was sent off to Mecca and died on the road near Damascus. Kamran was blinded after an attempt to ally himself with the Afghan ruler Islam Shah, son of Sher Shah, in 1552, and then sent off to Mecca as well. He died in Arabia in 1557.

When Humayun and Hamida Banu Begam made their way through Sistan, Khurasan, and Fars, ostensibly to travel to the Hijaz and perform the hajj, but more immediately to solicit support from the Persian emperor in a planned attempt to regain Hindustan, Akbar was one year and three months old and about to be separated from his parents for two years. The royal couple hurried off "through a desert and waterless waste" in extremely hot weather, leaving Akbar in the care and tutelage of his uncle Askari. By all accounts the separation from his parents and the subsequent period of custody was an unhappy time for Akbar, although Abu-l-Fazl points out that he did not make his misery manifest – already then showing great restraint. Little Akbar was placed in a camel litter and delivered into the care of Askari's wife, Sultan Begam, in Qandahar on December 16, 1543. He later claimed to be able to recall everything that happened to him in this period of his life with perfect accuracy. He remembered how he began to walk, for example, and how his guardian Askari struck him with his turban in order to make him fall, according to Turkish custom. He also claimed to remember that it was taken as good luck for him to have his head shaved at the shrine of Baba Hasan Abdal, in the western outskirts of Qandahar.

In 1544 Humayun returned to lay siege to Qandahar with Persian auxiliary troops (under the nominal command of the six-month-old

Persian prince Murad), and Askari decided to have Akbar, together
with his half-sister, conveyed to Kabul in the depth of winter. The
plan was that they would travel incognito – Akbar was called "Mirak"
on this journey and his half-sister "Bija" – but such were the marks of
Akbar's future greatness, we are assured, that the "nursling of light"
was always immediately recognized by the people they encountered
on the way. When Qandahar fell to Humayun's Persian troops, Akbar
was arriving in Kabul and about to be handed over to Khanazada
Begam, a sister of the late emperor Babur. She is described as having
been extremely fond of him, not least because he closely resembled
Babur. But Akbar's time in the harem was drawing to a close. In an age
when people saw omens everywhere, it was considered a bad omen
for Kamran that, in a publicly staged wrestling match, Akbar should
fling down his cousin Mirza Ibrahim, the slightly older son of
Kamran. Abu-l-Fazl would later proclaim this to be "the beginning of
the beating of the drum of victory and conquest of His Majesty" (AN,
I, 456). But the result was that Akbar was removed from the harem,
and kept under guard outside. Soon afterwards, in 1545, when
Humayun captured Kabul without a fight, he was re-united with his
parents. His circumcision was celebrated in the same audience hall
garden where the ladies of the harem had rejoiced over Babur's victory at Panipat in 1526.

But for Akbar things were to get worse before they would get better. This was due to the still stubborn resistance of at least two of
Humayun's brothers, which was now aggravated by the distractions
caused by another remaining Timurid, Mirza Sulayman, whose kingdom of Badakhshan (the mountainous region of northeast
Afghanistan today) had been restored to him by Babur in 1530 and
who was to remain a threat to Kabul long after Akbar had come to the
throne. For about half a decade Humayun was sidetracked by campaigns in Badakhshan, letting Kabul slip out of his hands and having to
recover it by force at least twice. The chronicles describe with horror
how on one of these occasions Akbar, effectively a hostage in enemy
hands, was used as a human shield, held up in front of the guns,
arrows, and lances of his own father.

AKBAR'S EDUCATION

Around 1551, at long last Humayun's position among his Timurid rivals was solidifying. At the same time, Akbar was being groomed for the succession and what would be his own – at that time still unforeseen – meteoric rise to power. He was about nine years old when he was given the government of the village of Carkh, in the tuman or "district" of Lahugar. His uncle Hindal died when he was ten years old, and he was given charge of Hindal's servants and retinue, together with all the latter's revenue assignments (jagirs). Akbar's destiny was now becoming manifest, for these assignments included the town of Ghazna, the former capital of Sultan Mahmud of Ghazna and the so-called "Ghaznavid" dynasty which in the late tenth and eleventh centuries had acquired unrivaled fame as the first Muslim conquerors of Hindustan. The more practical aim of this administrative promotion was that "by the practice of rule, he [Akbar] might exhibit favor and severity in the management of men; and by administration of a part, he might become accustomed to administer the whole" (AN, I, 596). Akbar spent six months in Ghazna, from the end of November 1551 to the end of May 1552, "in order that his greatness might be tested . . . [and] that all might know his abilities, and also that he might have practice in the art of rule" (AN, I, 596).

In November 1554, when Humayun set out for the re-conquest of Hindustan, Akbar was twelve years and eight months old. It was a conquest that was to be regarded as both a temporal and a spiritual victory, and Humayun ordered that it be inscribed in Akbar's name, indicating thereby that Akbar was nominally in command of the entire campaign. By now the Afghan empire in Hindustan was irretrievably fragmenting, with three different khutbas or "Friday prayers" being read at the same time in the names of three contesting sovereigns. Arriving at the town of Sirhind, in the Panjab, Akbar was given a tutor, Khwaja Ambar Nazir, an old servant of the family who was called from Kabul to explain to him "the manners and customs of India, and who brought Indians before the Unique of the Age" (AN, I, 629). Soon afterwards, when Humayun entered Delhi on July 24,

1555, and established himself on the imperial throne, Akbar was given an opportunity to gain first-hand experience of military command. The military training of Mughal princes – in archery, swordsmanship, horse-riding, and wrestling – began so early and was so intensive that it was not uncommon for them to undertake their first military commands while still in their teens. Babur was a military commander at the age of twelve. Humayun went on his first military campaign (to Badakhshan) when he was eleven. Akbar did so at the age of thirteen. On Humayun's orders he was sent out to prepare a safe route which the royal harem was to take from Kabul through the Panjab and keep the remaining Afghans at bay in the northern hills. While in the Panjab, Akbar was instructed in artillery by the best available Ottoman tutor, Rumi Khan.

In addition to the thorough military training he received in his early youth, Akbar had drawing lessons with distinguished Persian painters. He also learned "every breathing and sound that appertains to the Hindi language" (Tuzuk, I, 150), in all probability (although we cannot be sure) before he ascended the throne; and he developed a strong interest in the composition of Hindi as well as Persian poetry early on. But he grew up illiterate. Early attempts to teach him to read and write failed from the very beginning. Instruction was scheduled to begin, again at an astrologically propitious hour, when he was four years, four months, and four days old (November 20, 1547), but the future emperor failed even to show up. His first private tutor merely succeeded in communicating to him a taste for pigeon flying. A second tutor proved equally ineffectual. Or so it was said, but there is evidence that Akbar may have been dyslectic and that his learning disabilities caused both tutors to be dismissed as incompetent. A third tutor discharged his duties as best he could for some years, then chose to retire to Mecca.

As a child, Akbar displayed far greater interest in outdoor sports, and in animals, particularly camels (because they were the largest animals in the region) and Arabian horses. He also liked, apart from pigeon flying, hunting with dogs. His father Humayun admonished him with kind words, and even sent some poetry of his own to motivate the boy to study. It was to no avail. A courtier sent after the wayward prince found him lying in the grass, looking serene, as if he were asleep, but in fact "contemplating his plans for world conquest." For Abu-l-Fazl this episode demonstrated once again that "the lofty comprehension of this Lord of the Age was not learned or acquired, but was the gift of God in which human effort had no part" (AN, I, 589) – an assessment we may regard as a sixteenth-century form of spin.

Functional illiteracy in all likelihood stimulated Akbar to develop other skills, including the kind of practical skills that his great-grand-son Aurangzeb – so much the opposite of Akbar in other ways – was also to value. For example, he was later to master the skills of crafts-men, including carpentry, and took great pride and pleasure in them. His illiteracy no doubt also forced him to develop his already out-standing memory.

When he was about fifteen or sixteen, and already in his third year as king, he was introduced to the mystical writings of Hafiz by a Persian tutor from Qazwin. The latter's son appears to have been appointed to put Akbar through some sort of remedial educational program that included the refinement of manners, historical know-ledge, all subjects of conversation, and poetry, but Akbar continued to show little scholastic aptitude throughout his youth. Father Monserrate, a Jesuit who attended Akbar's court in the early 1580s, would comment that Akbar was "uneducated . . . [but] famous for his warlike skill and courage" (Monserrate, 34). According to the same writer, Akbar was "entirely unable to read or write" (Monserrate, 201). It is independently confirmed by others. Akbar was described as "illiterate" by his own son and successor Jahangir (Tuzuk, I, 33).

It was a condition, a "deficiency," uncommon among Mughal princes, not to say unique. We know that in Mughal times the princes were normally taught to read and write in their own Turkic language when they reached the age of five, and that they were apprenticed in the liberal arts with the same strictness as they were in the military arts. By the time they left the palace, at the age of sixteen, they would have been taught all the typical virtues of ruling elites, such as equanimity and prudence, as well as the useful knowledge of legal argumentation and dispassionate and impartial judgment. Akbar is known to have taken his own sons through such an education (which comprised Koranic instruction as well), not allowing the fatigues of travel to interrupt it even for a single day. Mughal princesses also virtually always learned to read and write, and they received a genuine literary education before they were put through finishing school under specially appointed matrons.

But if Akbar remained illiterate and his learning disabilities initially did cause consternation, there was no lasting shame attached to this condition. Observing that the prophets – Muhammad included – had been illiterate, Akbar went so far as to recommend that believers retain one of their sons in that condition, thus making a virtue of his deficiency. Timur, his revered ancestor, he pointed out, had been illiterate too. And, needless to say, most people in Akbar's time were illiterate. In the region of Kabul, where Akbar grew up, the local Afghans would merely be sent to a mulla for education in their infancy. From him they would learn the regular devotional and certain other prayers, as well as some passages from the Koran (sometimes in Arabic without understanding it), certain ceremonies, and their duties as Muslims. If we can go by late-eighteenth-century estimates, not more than a quarter of the Afghans could read and write their own language. Even the brahmans of India more often than not could not read or write. Of course, the education of a prince was a different matter. Nonetheless, Akbar managed well enough without these skills since, like the illiterate kings of medieval Europe, he was always assisted by hordes of clerks.

It should thus not be concluded, on the basis of the poor scholastic performance of the young Akbar, that he held literacy, or even clerical work, in disguised or undisguised contempt or was indifferent to it. To be sure, such an attitude of contempt was not unknown in his day. It was, in effect, widespread among the illiterate Rajput princes, as well as among such warlike tribes as the Yusufzai Afghans of the plains (who regarded the very activity of reading as unmanly). Akbar, when he grew into maturity, developed an

extraordinary – extraordinary in a ruler – taste for philosophy, theology, and religion, and was eager to have history recounted for him.
Not only did he take the literary education of his own children very
seriously (none of them was left illiterate), but he became a great
patron of higher learning, and apparently owned a library.
Monserrate described Akbar as a man of excellent judgment and
good memory who had attained a considerable erudition in many
fields by listening to others, and who outshone his subjects not only
in authority and dignity, as befitted a king, but often also in elo-
quence. Monserrate added that "no one who did not know that he is
illiterate would suppose him to be anything but very learned and eru-
dite" (Monserrate, 201). This particular quality of Akbar is also high-
lighted by his son Jahangir, who writes in his memoirs that: "My
father always associated with the learned of every creed and religion,
especially with Pandits and the learned of India, and although he was
illiterate, so much became clear to him through constant intercourse
with the learned and the wise, and in his conversations with them,
that no one knew him to be illiterate, and he was so acquainted with
the niceties of prose and verse composition that this deficiency was
not thought of" (Tuzuk, I, 33).

2

AN OLD WORLD GREW
YOUNG

When, on March 10, 1556, Akbar was raised to the Mughal throne in the town of Kalanaur, a suburb of the capital city of Lahore, at the age of fourteen, it was the beginning of a reign that would prove, in more than one way, to be unique, or at least highly uncommon, in Indo-Islamic history. He came to power at a very young age as an illiterate prince. He would rule for almost half a century (in this he was rivaled only by his great-grandson Aurangzeb). And he was, moreover, not critically challenged by sibling rivalry.

There is another reason why Akbar stood out among the Great Mughals. In the first seven years of his reign he was not his own master but, on account of his young age, subordinated to a regent. As a result of his extensive practical, above all military, training, Akbar was not wholly unprepared to succeed his father when the latter died unexpectedly in 1556, barely a year after the re-conquest of Hindustan. By universal consensus he was too young to rule independently, however, and Bairam Khan, the influential nobleman who had so successfully mediated Humayun's stay in Iran, officially became regent of the reconstituted Mughal dominion, charged with plenipotentiary powers for an indefinite time. After four years, Bairam Khan had to cede these powers to Maham Anga, a woman who owed her influential position, at least in part, to her former status as Akbar's chief wet-nurse. The position of wet-nurse was one of considerable importance, since the wet-nurse's own sons became foster-brothers of the future sovereign. Maham Anga reinforced her position and extended her influence further by her shrewd manipulation of factional support for the advancement to high rank and military command of her son Adham Khan. She was Akbar's regent for three more years.

Like the English Regency, these seven years were a time of scandals and conspicuous consumption among the nobles (most notably among the regents and their allies themselves) who were part of Akbar's court-in-the-making. It was also a time of great political flux, in which still powerful competitors for the throne of Hindustan, above all the Afghans and their Hindu allies, but also relatively minor rulers like the Timurid Mirza Sulayman of Badakhshan, made their presence felt. We can see clearly, nonetheless, how Akbar gradually came into his own as a ruler during these first seven regency years of his reign and how his dominion grew in size.

The regency notwithstanding, from the very beginning of the first year of his reign the Friday prayers were read in Akbar's name, even in Delhi, although that city was hardly secured and slipped out of Mughal hands again in the same year. Likewise, from the beginning of the regency years, high-sounding ancestral titles were adopted for Akbar, like Padshah ("emperor") or Shahanshah ("king of kings"). Later tradition has in fact always regarded the regency years as an integral part of Akbar's reign. When in 1584 Akbar introduced a new calendar, the so-called "Tarikh-i-Ilahi" or "Divine Era," the year of his accession, 1556, and not 1563, the year in which the regency came to an end, was retroactively turned into Year One.

The Mughal identification with India as a new "homeland" was still weak and developed but slowly. In 1561 Akbar made his first visit to the tomb of the great Indian Sufi saint Mu'in ad-Din Chishti in Ajmer – the most important cult object of Indian Muslims of the time. In the same year he entered the first of his many marriages, to a Hindu woman belonging to a Rajput lineage which was probably older than his own. Mughal architecture was still almost non-existent. Babur had laid out gardens in several important places, and he and his nobles built three mosques in the subcontinent, including the Kabuli

Bagh mosque at the historic battlefield of Panipat. Babur's grave was and remained in Kabul, still unmarked and uncovered, overgrown merely with wild flowers (in conformity with his last wishes). Humayun's citadel at Delhi, which was named Din Panah ("Refuge of Religion") by him and which is known as Purana Qila, had been completed by the Afghan ruler Sher Shah. Humayun had been buried in an improvised shrine at Sirhind, in the Panjab, from where he was later moved to the magnificent sandstone mausoleum in Delhi which we now associate with his name and which was built between 1563 and 1572. Akbar himself spent five months of the year 1556, including the entire rainy season, in a muddy camp at Jalandhar, also in the Panjab, and it was here that he received the first foreign ambassadors (from Kashghar) who came to congratulate him on his accession. Jalandhar remained the new emperor's base until he moved to Lahore and then back to Delhi in December 1557, shortly after it was retaken. The fort of Delhi was not strengthened until 1560.

In October 1558 Akbar moved his entire entourage by boat to Agra, a city which is described by contemporary sources as having a more temperate climate than Delhi, and was renowned for its fruit-trees. He made that city his capital, partly for these reasons, and partly because it was easier to extend his conquests from here to the Afghan-held territories of Malwa, Lakhnau, and Jaunpur. In Agra, the Mughal nobles began to erect mansions and gardens, while Akbar moved into an old and ruinous brick citadel known as Badalgarha, on the eastern side of the Yamuna. The construction of the Red Fort was not taken in hand until 1565, and did not reach completion until eight years afterwards. A great deal of military campaigning still had to be done before Humayun's harem could be safely conveyed to Agra.

Humayun's dowager and "chaste ladies" were still in Kabul – the city that had really remained the Timurid-Mughal capital. Here Mirza Muhammad Hakim, Akbar's younger half-brother, was the nominal ruler and like Akbar himself under a regent, while the Friday prayers were read in Akbar's name and also (once in 1556, in the presence of merely a few people, and only "outwardly, not inwardly") in the name of Mirza Sulayman, the Timurid ruler of Badakhshan, who was asserting himself militarily in the area. Some of the most important nobles, like the regent Bairam Khan, still had their revenue holdings in Qandahar and other places west of the Indus. The territories further east were in fact a military frontier. There, in the Siwaliks, in Delhi, in the Panjab, and in Rajasthan, Gwalior, Malwa, and Awadh, incessant campaigns had to be conducted against Afghan warlords of the ancien regime, who retained major strongholds like Chunar, as well as against Hindu rulers, often ensconced in hill forts, or against combinations of both.

Not all Hindu opposition to Akbar originated among the ancient Rajput nobility. The decisive showdown of the regency years was with Hemu, a Hindu general of the Afghans who was apparently of quite modest, almost "outcaste" background, and who had entered Delhi to set himself up as an independent ruler under the Hindu title of Raja Vikramaditya. Akbar and Bairam Khan were lucky against Hemu's much superior forces and artillery. The Hindu general was struck in the eye by an arrow, which brought the engagement, at Panipat on November 5, 1556, to a quick end as the leaderless army was thrown into confusion. There are graphic descriptions of how Hemu's wife, after this defeat, tried to escape to the hills with the accumulated treasure of decades of Afghan rule loaded on pack elephants, leaving a trail of gold coins and ingots in her wake (travelers would continue to find them for years afterwards), and of how she ultimately had to abandon the elephants along with the remaining treasure to the villagers and the army sent in pursuit of her. Hemu's headless trunk was sent to Delhi and there placed on a gibbet as a dire warning. His head was sent to Kabul and hung on the iron gate there.

It was not until then that the harem of Humayun and the families of many household officials considered the situation safe enough to set out in cortege toward India, with only Mirza Muhammad Hakim and his family staying on in Kabul. Akbar lost two of his sisters on this journey. But the cortege reached Jalandhar, where Akbar went out to welcome them. It was another milestone in the Mughal conquest of Hindustan. As Abu-l-Fazl explained, Akbar gave the order "to fetch their highnesses, the Begams, and the families of the servants of the household and bring them into the delightful and extensive lands of India from Kabul, so that men might become settled and be restrained in some measure from departing to a country to which they were accustomed" (AN, II, 30–31). Other immigrants followed suit, as they did after every other military triumph of significance. Akbar was still spending most of his time hunting or watching elephant fights, but the faith in his emerging dominion was growing, and "although the ruler of the age was spending his days under the veil of indifference, yet every day men of genius and talent, loyal combatants, devoted heroes, sages, and other men of skill were coming from the quarters of the earth in troops and were gaining their desires" (AN, I, 122).

Keeping in check the warriors who executed his early conquests was difficult enough, requiring constant vigilance, including "hunting tours" to thwart any number of potential defections among old retainers and new recruits alike; but on balance the regency years, for Akbar, were a "dominion-increasing time." Bairam Khan, the regent, in sharp contrast, "became a traveler on a roadless tract." Whether the latter ever really aspired to the throne himself is difficult to make out, but there are signs that he did. Already in the second year he began distributing the royal elephants among his confidential officers, and even seized some of them for himself. Akbar regarded this as an encroachment upon a royal prerogative, but although he did not wish to submit to it he decided to postpone action against it until, by the fourth year, Bairam Khan's position was irremediably troubled. The regent had begun acting as if the affairs of India could not be managed without him. It was now intimated to Akbar that the time had come to assume sovereignty for himself. When it came to light that Bairam Khan had been contemplating an alliance with some of the "black-hearted and short-sighted" Afghans and harbored designs of taking Lahore, some even urged war against him. For the time being Akbar acquiesced in Maham Anga, his former wet-nurse, taking charge of affairs. Bairam Khan himself chose to leave Agra on April 8, 1560, imagining he could enter the

Panjab — which was "a mine of resources" — unhindered, while pretending to go to Mecca. His path, however, was blocked by troops loyal to Akbar, followed by his final climb-down, his acceptance of a robe of honor that had been worn by the emperor himself, and then his being granted final "permission" to proceed to Mecca. Setting out for this destination, he was assassinated by a group of Afghans in Pattan, Gujarat, with the words "Allahu Akbar" on his lips.

The regency troubles were by now nearly over, although not quite. Maham Anga, the former wet-nurse, was still maneuvering on behalf of Adham Khan, her younger son, who was also Akbar's foster-brother, and who was passed over for the position of chief minister. When Adham Khan appeared to become hostile, Akbar threw him from a terrace in his palace — twice, to make sure he died. Maham Anga died of grief forty days later. Like Bairam Khan, the second regent and her son were both given honorable funerals, the first in the Shi'ite capital of Mashhad in eastern Iran, and the latter two in Delhi. Akbar personally escorted the body of Maham Anga "for some paces," and he ordered a lofty building to be erected over their tombs.

3

THE DAILY INCREASING
DOMINION

Abu-l-Fazl devotes some fifty or sixty pages of the *Akbarnama* to the auspicious horoscope that was cast at Akbar's birth (AN, I, 69–128). When he was born, the smile on his face was "the opening bud of hope and peace" (AN, I, 132). At Akbar's accession to the throne in 1556 another horoscope was cast, announcing that his dominion would "daily increase and prosper"(AN, II, 10–14). Forty years later, in the closing decade of the great century, a historian of Akbar's later reign, Shaykh Abdul Haqq, wrote that Akbar was "still in the bloom of his dominion, even though he has been on the throne for more than forty years . . . For every day brings accounts of new victories and new conquests, so that by the blessing of God his kingdom extends over the whole of Hindustan (which is called 'chahardang', that is, a quarter of the world), east and west, north and south, including all its forts and territories, without anyone being associated with him in power, and without anyone daring to offer opposition"(ED,VI, 180–181).

The beneficent monarch is depicted as being ever intent on conquest – but only to liberate the oppressed from the tyranny of other rulers, we are assured. As Abu-l-Fazl writes: "In conquering countries and cities his first thought is to inquire into and sympathize with the condition of the oppressed" (AN, II, 536). Akbar's conquest of Gujarat in 1572 was justified because "the oppression of the subjects there had reached its climax" (AN, II, 537). In the following year,

1573, "the Shahanshah addressed himself to the conquest of Bihar and Bengal because the peasantry were suffering from the dominion of the evil Afghans" (AN, III, 57). And on the eve of the conquest of the Deccan in 1585, "His Majesty's sole idea was to give tranquillity to the feeble ones of the Deccan, and to improve the rulers thereof. If they would not administer justice and cherish their people they were to be properly punished" (AN, III, 701).

This is evidently a propagandistic mode of representation, routinely adopted by the chief court historians of Akbar's reign. Any opponents of Akbar are cast in the role of evil tyrants and oppressors. The latter included, at times, his own Mughal nobles. These were almost all high-born individuals, recruited from the Irano-Turanian lands outside the subcontinent, who perpetually kept their own interests at heart, and some of whom broke into open rebellion. Prominent among those who rebelled against Akbar were the Uzbek nobles, belonging to a tribe which had been Babur's nemesis half a century earlier and which was still powerful in Balkh, Khurasan, Bukhara, and Farghana, and members of which had entered Akbar's service, albeit half-heartedly. A second prominent category of Mughal nobles who rebelled against Akbar were Timurids such as his half-brother Mirza Muhammad Hakim and other "Mirzas" in Hindustan and later Gujarat. (Mirza was a Timurid title derived from *mirzada* or "son of a prince.") There were many others among the Mughal nobles who, individually or in groups, offered opposition to Akbar, either openly or in more covert ways (by delaying operations, conspiring with the enemy, double-dealing, obstruction, sabotage, and so on), even though they were formally in his service. To some extent, such obstruction among the Mughal nobility was the normal state of affairs.

Outside the Mughal nobility, Akbar's opponents included, most prominently, the numerous Afghan warlords – generally described as "evil and black-fated" – with their Indian soldiers, who remained powerful in large parts of Hindustan, Malwa, and Gujarat, and in Bihar and Bengal, as well as in other places – the leftover of the ancien regime, now hopelessly fragmented. Further, there was the Rajput nobility of Rajasthan, and there were also innumerable small Hindu kings everywhere, and, mostly ensconced in the hills, major tribal confederacies such as the Gakkars in the Panjab or the Gonds of Gondwara. Akbar also came up against one major Muslim state that had been created in the early fifteenth century in the wake of Timur's destruction of Delhi and which had survived intact into the sixteenth century. This was the powerful Sultanate of Gujarat, founded by the dynasty of the Ahmad Shahs, with their capital at Ahmadabad. It was a rich agricultural state which, with access to the Arabian Sea, had great commercial importance and counted Surat, the gateway to Mecca, among its wealthy ports.

Overall, it is evident from the chronicles that Akbar's dominion increased but slowly and that it took immense efforts over four decades to consolidate it in the various parts of northern, western, and eastern India. But increasing it was, even though there were many setbacks, both military and political.

THE MUGHAL ARMY

The key to Mughal military success is to be found in the use of cavalry, more specifically the mounted archers, who were recruited from the same geographical regions as the nobility but in much larger numbers. Contemporary authors, without exception, make this same observation. Monserrate, for instance, already asserts correctly that "the strength of the Tartar [i.e. Mughal] armies lies in their cavalry . . . organized in accordance with the system of Cinguiscanus [Latin for 'Chingis Khan']" (Monserrate, 68). We also have to take into account that the Mughals controlled the regular supply of superior "Turki" warhorses from the steppe lands – and that this was an advantage they held over all Indian rulers, as also over the Afghans (who, after all, had lost control of Kabul, the major entrepôt of the horse trade), although less so over the Sultans of Gujarat – the latter having access to a supply of "seaborne" horses from Persia and Arabia that was of a similarly high quality although probably smaller.

The central importance of mounted archery in Mughal warfare is in evidence from the beginning. When Humayun returned to India, the very first victory over the Afghans, in the battle at Machiwara, on the banks of the Sutlej, was entirely gained by mounted archers. The latter remained the main asset of the Mughal military, expanding in total numbers from about 12,000 in the mid-sixteenth century to 100,000 and more in the late seventeenth. Most of these came from Iran and Turan (Central Asia), and often, though not necessarily, had a nomadic background. The Mughals preferred to recruit their cavalry in these regions outside the subcontinent because they produced the best-trained military men, mounted on the best warhorses, and, moreover, the recruits from these regions could be expected to remain relatively detached from Indian society as they had no roots in the soil. The Mughal dynasty did not resort to the use of military slaves (mamluks) – quite unlike many, if not most, other prominent Islamic dynasties in medieval and early modern times – but the de-racinated horse warriors they did employ were in some essential respects similar to the "slaves on horses" used elsewhere. The Mughals recruited them in the way mercenaries are normally recruited, that is to say as bands already formed, led by their own amirs or "commanders," who had put them together, often from their own homelands, and they were paid in cash, while the amirs themselves held high ranks or "mansabs" in the Mughal military-bureaucratic apparatus, in effect constituting the nobility. Almost from the beginning, the entire Mughal army was under the command of a few hundred of such high-ranking amirs. Later, particularly in the seventeenth century, the latter were increasingly born in India, like much of their retinue, but they never became a landholding aris-tocracy with Indian roots. This was due to their peculiar mode of remuneration of their amirs which the Mughals adopted from their Indo-Islamic predecessors and which remained almost until the end a system of strictly temporary and often non-contiguous revenue assignments, divorced from governmental power, rotating through-out the empire (see Chapter 6).

Under Akbar, the cavalry forces continued to be made up

overwhelmingly of immigrant rather than Indian-born recruits. The subjected Indian warrior castes like the Rajputs became important in the Mughal army to the extent that they conformed to the new style of cavalry warfare. This took some time because it required a profound transformation of earlier Rajput military practices and the entire ethos that went with it. In the early sixteenth century, and in some places long afterwards, the Rajputs were still feudal in their outlook. They carried only swords and short spears or lances into war, with light shields, nothing like bows and arrows or fire-arms that could kill from a dishonorable distance. Before the beginning of a battle, they were almost always heavily drugged with opium. The medieval Rajputs strove to win or die with their archaic sense of honor intact. They did not have access to large warhorses, and often rode on ponies hardly as big as donkeys, dismounting for battle. Akbar immediately set out to change this pattern of Rajput warfare when he co-opted the leading Rajput warlords in his imperial service. Like the foreign Muslim amirs, the Rajput warlords then began to employ their own kinsmen as well as non-kin retainers and, with better horses, organized them into cavalry units that, already under Akbar, played a secondary but important role in Mughal warfare. Beyond the Rajputs, the Mughals understood and used to their advantage the enormous military potential of the Indian countryside generally. As Abu-l-Fazl put it, there were 4.4 million "military men" in India. This number referred to Hindu soldiers of a great variety, in the service of local rulers and landlords, or tribal militias and the like. Although they were no match for the descendants of Chingis Khan and Timur, these "peasant soldiers," rooted in local society, did find employment, mostly as infantry in the Mughal army, and with strength in numbers, they too played a significant role in a range of circumstances.

The Mughal cavalry under Akbar, however, itself represented the culmination of a revolution in warfare which had begun, centuries earlier, under his Indo-Muslim predecessors and which had been responsible for increasingly driving out Indian peasant armies, the disorderly infantries of hundreds of thousands, as well as the related, logistically complex, elephant warfare of medieval times (which was only suitable for set battles) throughout the subcontinent. The Mughal cavalry maneuvered with great ease, even though it was clad in iron armor, and discharged its arrows with astonishing speed. Mughal horsemen could shoot arrows six times in the time it took musketeers to fire twice. On campaigns they would each be accompanied by about four to five servants or slaves (ghulams) on foot; in a reversal these would flee and rush about in a panic, unable to provide any assistance to their masters, but the Mughal cavalry itself always preserved excellent order, and kept together in a compact body, especially when charging the enemy. Among the soldiers of the ordinary and petty Hindu rajas, the fear of the Mughal cavalry was such that forty thousand of them would not stand against two thousand horsemen. Those rag-tag armies, still consisting almost exclusively of infantry, marched in long disorderly files, their wives and children in tow, carrying some spears or a matchlock, and with baskets of cooking-pots and pans on their heads.

If they did not have warhorses, none of the Hindu rulers that Akbar encountered, not even the pre-eminent Rajputs, appears to have possessed any artillery whatsoever, although some of the smaller Muslim rulers like the Arghuns of Sind and the Afghan warlords and their Hindu generals did (Sher Shah was killed by a malfunctioning artillery piece of his own), and the Sultans of Gujarat had a grand park of artillery and mortars, some of which had been obtained directly from the Ottoman Sultan Sulayman the Magnificent – this was another reason, in addition to their access to warhorses, why they were such formidable opponents. Gunpowder weapons were still relatively new. In Hindustan they had made their appearance with Babur, and on the coasts, with the Portuguese, by the early decades of the sixteenth century. The skills and technology of gunpowder weapons were essentially passed on to the Mughals by the Ottoman-Turkish rulers of "Rum" (i.e. Constantinople, the "second Rome"), as well as by the Europeans. In effect, in the sixteenth century there was intense competition for such expertise and technology between all the major states from the Horn of Africa (where

Ottoman artillery emboldened a jihad against the Christian empire of Ethiopia) to the Hindu empire of Vijayanagara in South India, and to the emerging maritime Muslim powers of Johore and Aceh in the eastern Indian Ocean. Akbar himself, as we have seen, was trained in artillery shooting by a "Rumi Turk" (probably a man from Aleppo).

"Rumi Turks" and "Firangis" (i.e. "Franks" – some of them converts) remained much in demand for their brilliant pyrotechnic skills throughout the sixteenth century and the early decades of the seventeenth, after which we see their pay drop commensurately with the decreasing rarity value of their skills when these began to spread in India itself. Both groups were, without a doubt, a major factor in the success of Akbarian imperialism.

At first the artillery was still virtually immobile and mostly used in defense. An army would dig itself in, with carts tied together in the Turkish style, as Babur had done at Panipat. With artillery, this defensive position would be virtually unassailable. Spurred on by opponents like Sher Shah, as well as the latter's descendants, the Mughals appear to have lost no time in building up their artillery park. Humayun already boasted that "none but the Kaisar of Rum has artillery like ours" (TA, II, p. 50). In Akbar's time, artillery pieces, still mostly useless for siege purposes, were routinely carried along with the moving camps, or, if possible, floated down rivers on war boats. These field guns were typically grouped together in front of the camp, opposite the entrance of the royal quarters, and in the broadest part of the open ground. They went by the name of "artillery of the stirrup" and were never out of the emperor's sight, not even when he was searching for hunting grounds off the main road, or traveling along difficult passes (for example on the way to Kashmir, Akbar's favorite holiday destination), or crossing bridges of boats – unlike the heavy artillery, which did not always follow the king, although that too was dragged through rough terrain over great distances on carts and pack animals.

The most innovative of Akbar's policies was that of allying himself with the major Rajput princes. Ironically, this policy was inspired by the advice given to his father by Shah Tahmasp of Persia, a ruler notorious for his religious (i.e. Shi'ite) bigotry. The alliance with these princes was perhaps Akbar's most important political achievement but it did not come about without the prior application of force. Akbar's conquest of the pre-eminent Rajput dynasty's legendary stronghold of Chitor in 1567 was especially bloody and brutal, even by the standards of the time. Many of the other Rajputs were sufficiently intimidated by it to enter Akbar's service voluntarily and start paying him tribute in exchange for administrative autonomy within their clannish realms. It was perhaps more through the political agency than the sheer military might of the "infidel" Rajput princes that Akbar increased his dominion in the greater part of Hindustan. He did not restrict his alliances to a few famous Rajput houses, however, or even to the three hundred or so Hindu "rajas and landholders" that al-Qandahari says "wanted only friendly relations and came to attend the imperial court" (TAK, 67). Rather he made what some Islamic diehards in his entourage disparagingly referred to as "the Hindus" indispensable everywhere – in his army, administration, and court – by assigning them many of the highest positions and admitting them to the innermost parts of the palace. These relationships were strengthened by matrimonial ties.

Three factors therefore – mounted archery, artillery, and the alliance with the Rajputs – made the Mughals prevail in the second half of the sixteenth century. None of these was entirely new for the Mughal dynasty in India. Mounted archery and artillery had been brought to Hindustan by Babur. The idea of an alliance with the Rajputs had been suggested to Humayun. But Humayun's reign had been marred by the rivalry of his brothers and was then cut short by his premature death. It was thus left to Akbar to use these assets to full advantage.

THE CONQUEST OF GUJARAT

In the late 1560s, the principal rival of the budding Mughal polity under Akbar was the Sultanate of Gujarat, the fabulously wealthy maritime state of western India, which was now de facto governed by

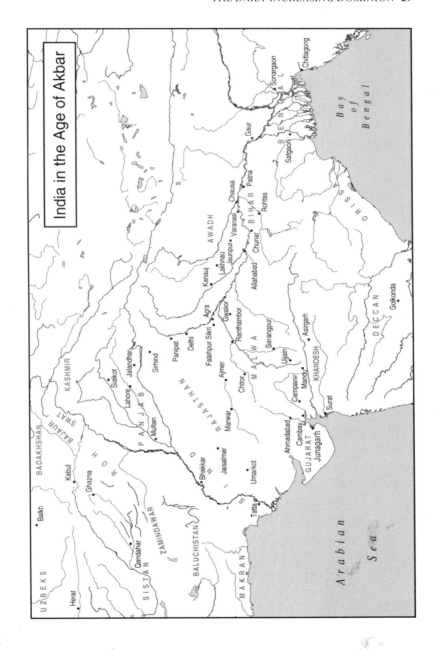

India in the Age of Akbar

an officer of the Ahmad Shahi dynasty of Mongol origin named Chingis Khan. With Akbar's dominion increasing in Hindustan, in Gujarat too "the demand for men of discrimination and excellence was such as to exceed all imagination," and recruitment as well as retention efforts reached a feverish pitch (MT, II, 67). It was the beginning of a prolonged contest for power between Akbar and the Gujarati dynasty which would continue intermittently until the final years of the century, when it was finally decided in Akbar's favor. The Mughal conquest of Gujarat was as much a political as a military struggle. Much of the time it was complicated by the fact that the Uzbeks in Akbar's service and the Timurid princes who were known as the "Mirzas" would switch sides at opportune moments, bringing Afghan warlords of the ancien regime along with them.

The Uzbek nobles in Akbar's service had, at first, helped him defeat the Afghans at Chunar but they soon began to resent his self-aggrandizing power, as also his employment of Irani Shi'ite nobles. Not surprisingly, "suspicion of the whole Uzbek tribe found access to the emperor's mind"(MT, III, 74). The Uzbeks, in an about-face, applied for help from the "black-fated" Afghans who by now had withdrawn to Bengal and held on to the fort of Rohtas in Bihar. Together they moved to take control of the whole country from Lakhnau to the bank of the Ganges. There they began to recite the Friday prayers in the name of Akbar's half-brother Mirza Muhammad Hakim. By 1567 some of Akbar's leading commanders were out to strike a deal with these "rebels" ("They did not want the rebels to be disposed of until their own ends had been served," wrote Abu-l-Fazl (AN, II, 427)), and this prompted Akbar to move to this arena in person. By the time of his arrival the Uzbeks had been joined by the "Mirzas." The leader of the Mirzas was a descendant of Timur's second son (while Akbar descended from the third son), who was considered to have a good claim on the Mughal throne, especially as he also had marriage ties with Timurid princesses from Akbar's line. The Uzbeks' alliance with the Mirzas ultimately failed "for everyone in his folly wanted to rule [himself]" (AN, II, 413). With the Uzbeks following in disarray, the Mirzas moved on to Malwa, and then fled to

Gujarat, to join the growing ranks of men surrounding Chingis Khan, the de-facto ruler of Gujarat. The latter, however, died soon thereafter, leaving the Sultanate of Gujarat entirely to the Mirzas.

In 1572 Akbar set out to subdue the Mirzas who had seized power in Gujarat after the death of Chingis Khan. They were flushed out of Gujarat fairly quickly, in 1573, but continued to create disturbances in the province from a new base in the Deccan (the high plateau of Central India which remained mostly unconquered in Akbar's time) until as late as 1577. In 1583 a new rebellion flared up in the province when a descendant of the Gujarati dynasty, Muzaffar, assumed power again and plundered Cambay. Time and again the armies sent by Akbar to Gujarat displayed "cowardice and double-facedness" toward the enemy. Having had to return to Gujarat in person a second time in 1573, Akbar went there a third time in 1583. Sultan Muzaffar of Gujarat held out until as late as 1592, when he was finally captured and a remaining sixteen ports in the province were taken (including Junagarh, Somnath, and Soreth). After the latter's death, his son Bahadur raised commotions in Gujarat until as late as 1599.

Gujarat was the most powerful rival Sultanate in India in Akbar's time, with military advantages in terms of access to warhorses and artillery which were comparable to those of the Mughals. It was not conquered once and for all in 1572, when Akbar first moved there, but rather won in a long contest for power that evolved over more than three decades. The significance of this conquest was manifold. Not only did it eliminate the Mughals' most powerful single rival and provide further advantages to the Mughals in the acquisition of warhorses and artillery, it also added immensely to their agricultural revenues, and, perhaps most importantly, provided access to seaborne trade and supplies of precious metals that entered India through the commercial enclaves established here by the Portuguese. As we will see (chapter 6), precious metals – in particular silver – obtained by the Portuguese from the New World mines, as also from Africa and Japan, and exchanged in trade, were an essential factor in the development of all major Mughal institutions in the later sixteenth century.

KABUL, THE NORTH-WEST FRONTIER, AND THE "GREAT GAME" OF THE SIXTEENTH CENTURY

The control of Kabul and the North-West Frontier of the subcontinent became a second, almost lifelong preoccupation for Akbar. Kabul, beyond the Khyber pass and surrounded by mountains, has always been difficult to reach from the Indian plains. Yet Kabul – like Qandahar or "Zabulistan" – belonged to the Mughal dominion of India from its inception, whereas the lands beyond the Panjshir pass across the Hindu Kush mountains, comprising Balkh and often Badakhshan, belonged to the Uzbek dominion of Central Asia. Until 1585 Akbar's half-brother Mirza Muhammad Hakim retained the Kabul throne with the help of the Panjab troops. His position was ambivalent in that he now supported Akbar, now conspired with the Uzbeks against his more powerful brother, and intermittently also with the Timurid rulers of Badakhshan, and even the Mughal commanders of the Panjab in Akbar's service.

Geography ensured that whoever ruled Kabul was the major resource for all the disaffected Muslim elements in India. Akbar had the greatest difficulty keeping it under control. He had to go to Kabul in person to prevent his empire from being subverted from there by his half-brother Mirza Muhammad Hakim. After the latter's death he had to protect it from the Uzbeks of Balkh, who, he feared, would use it as their base for an invasion of Hindustan. The resulting Mughal-Uzbek standoff on the North-West Frontier resembles an early version of the "Great Game," the struggle between Russia and Victorian Britain for the mastery of these same borderlands.

Mughal historians unanimously assert that "there was no inborn goodness in Mirza Muhammad Hakim." The confrontation with Akbar began in 1580, when Akbar's introduction of new administrative and religious measures triggered a great rebellion among the Mughal officers in Bihar and Bengal (see "The conquest of Bengal" below). The rebels made an attempt to bring Mirza Muhammad Hakim from Kabul, to proclaim him emperor of Hindustan, and by way of preparation read the Friday prayers in his name, while loudly raising the cry of Islam in danger. As Monserrate wrote on the eve of these events: "One thing only was needed [to promote a general revolt], namely that all should judge it their duty and interest to engage in a legitimate rebellion against the King [Akbar], on behalf of their religion and their liberty" (Monserrate, 69–70). Mirza Muhammad Hakim, in effect, crossed the Indus river with 15,000 Mughal cavalry and arrived near Lahore. But when Akbar approached (under the pretext of "hunting"), even the traitors in the Panjab who had invited the Mirza would not stand by their promises. Humiliated, the latter had to swim back across the river in a hurry. Akbar then moved against his half-brother in full force – with 50,000 cavalry, plus infantry, and supplies of gold and silver.

On this occasion a beginning was made with the building of the fortress of Atak – to serve as "a noble barrier between Hindustan and Kabulistan" on the bank of the Indus. Akbar successfully moved through the difficult defile of the Khyber and had the satisfaction of sitting on the ancestral Mughal throne of Kabul for a few days. Before he set out on his return journey, he pardoned Mirza Muhammad Hakim and re-invested him with the territory of Kabul and Zabulistan – lest he join the Uzbeks. The Mirza died in 1585, at the age of thirty-one, leaving sons too young to succeed him, and Akbar then handed Kabul to two of his Rajput officers.

After Mirza Muhammad Hakim died, Uzbek horsemen seized Badakhshan and made ready to attack Kabul. Serious disturbances also broke out in the Panjab, and in 1586 Akbar was compelled to move to Sialkot. The threat of an Uzbek invasion kept him in Lahore, and "hunting" in the Panjab, for much of the last fifteen years of the sixteenth century. He never got around to pursuing the Uzbek leaders in their own country, although it was on his agenda for a long time. In retrospect, the decision not to invade the Uzbek lands was probably a judicious one. Akbar's grandson Shah Jahan undertook "hunting" expeditions in this area from 1636 onward, in order to prepare for the final invasion of Balkh and Badakhshan – which, when launched in 1645, proved disastrous.

The Uzbeks, however, never ceased to be a danger, although they did not seize Kabul. Until the end of his reign Akbar remained tied up on the North-West Frontier in campaigns against the local Afghan tribesmen – the warlike and millenarian Afridi, Orakzai, Yusufzai, and Muhammadzai between the Khyber pass and Swat and Bajaur – in his efforts to prevent Kabul from falling into Uzbek hands and to keep the Khyber pass open, and passable for wheels. Whenever Akbar succeeded in subduing one or other of the huge tribal confederacies no matter how temporarily, the Uzbeks recoiled in fear, and closed the gates of Balkh. But Akbar made sure not to provoke his Central-Asian neighbors too much, and always turned down forward policies suggested to him by advisers who aimed at the subjugation of Balkh. Instead, he spent his time in Lahore and the Panjab to increase and consolidate his dominion as much as possible in the frontier areas of Khyber, Swat, and Bajaur, as also in Qandahar, Garmsir, and Zamindawar, and further south, in Sind, Makran, and Baluchistan, and, to the north, in Kashmir. Around 1596 he wrote to the Uzbek king that he intended to keep the Hindu Kush as the boundary between them. Still, in 1601, the Badakhshanis read the Friday prayers in Akbar's name.

THE CONQUEST OF BENGAL

Bengal was the third of the interlocked arenas of conflict in which Akbar was involved for most of his career. Long before the arrival of the Mughals, India's eastern province was known as "the house of revolt" and "the land where owing to the climate favoring the base, the dust of dissension is always rising." The supposed effects of the climate apart, Bengal's fragmented geography of jungles and innu-merable waterways provided the best possible hideout for the former Indo-Afghan rulers of Hindustan, now on the run but still commanding a considerable following.

The conquest of Bengal – and its adjacent provinces of Bihar and Orissa – was, like that of Gujarat, not a single event but a long-drawn effort to subdue the Afghans retaining power in these eastern provinces. The first military successes against these Afghans, in this particular case a group holding out in the fortress of Rohtas in Bihar, are recorded as early as 1564. Akbar's departure to Gujarat in 1572 emboldened them again. By 1574 the Afghan leader Daud, in possession of powerful artillery, had shut himself up in the fort of Patna, still in Bihar. Akbar then "realized that the conquest of Bihar and Bengal could not be accomplished without himself going there" (AN, III, 110). He thus set off, in the rainy season, and captured Patna. From this date the Afghans began to be driven further and further to the east, into the heart of Bengal, then further still, to Satgaon, Sonargaon, Orissa, and as far as Chittagong. Abu-l-Fazl proclaimed March 3, 1575, "the day of the conquest of that wide territory" (AN, III, 179). This was the day that Daud's severed head, stuffed with straw and anointed with perfumes in order not to trouble the emperor, was brought in. The fortress of Rohtas was also taken at this time. But the Mughal troops procrastinated when an epidemic broke out and the emperor's simultaneous reversals in Gujarat led to a temporary resurgence of Afghan resistance in 1577. In 1580 Akbar's officers in Bihar joined the Afghans in Bengal in the greatest rebellion of his reign. They distributed territories, honors, titles, and appointments in the name of Mirza Muhammad Hakim — the ruler of Kabul. In 1583 Bengal had to be "conquered for the third time," as Abu-l-Fazl put it. Akbar then built a great fortress at the junction of the Ganges and Yamuna, at what is now Allahabad. The so-called "twelve landholders" of Bengal also submitted to his rule. Orissa was conquered, and the eastern Afghans were finally driven into "the forests near the sea" in 1592. This happened at about the same time that the conquest of Gujarat was nearing completion and the Uzbeks on the North-West Frontier were effectively contained. Akbar's dominion had now reached its fullest extent.

4

CLOUDS AND ELEPHANTS
AND MUD

In the words of a nineteenth-century British historian, John William Kaye, the Mughal dynasty was "the most magnificent that the world had ever seen" (Kaye, 646). Whatever the value or truth of this judgment may be, it was not yet common in the sixteenth century. Monserrate, who was well acquainted with Akbar personally and traveled widely in the Mughal empire of the 1580s, is also appreciative, but rather more sober in his judgment: "The splendor of his palaces approaches closely to that of the royal dwellings in Europe. They are magnificently built, from foundation to cornice, of hewn stone, and are decorated both with painting and carving. Unlike the palaces built by other kings, they are lofty; for an Indian palace is generally as low and humble as an idol-temple . . . The other buildings erected by Zelaldinus [Jalal ad-Din, i.e. Akbar] in various parts of his dominions are of equal magnificence" (Monserrate, 199–200).

The real life of the Mughal emperors – especially the sixteenth-century ones – was in fact far from always an experience of barely imaginable luxury and extravagance. Like his father Humayun, and his grandfather Babur, and like some European kings of the time (for instance Charles V of Spain), Akbar spent much of his life traveling around, frequently in difficult and physically challenging circumstances. It was not until the seventeenth century – the reigns of Jahangir and Shah Jahan – that Mughal emperors became sybarites and began patronizing truly magnificent architecture and other forms of display. Even this much more lavish Mughal style barely lasted half a century. It was already over by the time Aurangzeb came to the throne. That emperor – the last of the Great Mughals – spent the final twenty-five years of his life in fruitless campaigns against an elusive enemy in the rocky tableland of the Deccan, amidst outbreaks of epidemics that could wipe out as much as a third of his army in just one week. Here Mughal resources were stretched thin. Manucci observed in 1700 that "it is now nineteen years that he [Aurangzeb] has been in camp without effecting anything against that rebellious people, the Marathas . . . Owing to the immense expenditure forced upon him, and because the revenue-payers did not pay with the usual promptitude, he was obliged at Aurangabad to melt down all his household silver ware" (Manucci, II, 239).

Much of the imperial traveling of Mughal times was prompted by the desire to keep recalcitrant officers – or brothers – on the side of loyalty, in other words to keep aspiring rebels from gaining too much traction in the areas of India yet to be subdued (or unsubduable) and thereby acquiring the ability to turn against the emperor. In the case of Akbar we have some vivid descriptions in the *Akbarnama* of the itinerant life he led for long periods from virtually his birth up to the eve of his death.

EPISODE ONE: 1564–1566

One episode began in the ninth year of his reign, in 1564, when Akbar received word that one of his Uzbek nobles, Abdullah Khan, had started a rebellion in Malwa (AN, II, 341–370). Akbar resolved to use the pretext of elephant hunting to undertake an expedition against him. He set out on July 2, when the monsoon had already begun and huge clouds (Abu-l-Fazl compares these to "proudly-stalking elephants") unleashed torrents of rain, causing furious floods which made it impossible to distinguish highlands from lowlands. When the imperial camp was pitched on the bank of the Chambal, a halt of two weeks was ordered to enable the entire army to cross the river – which was in full flood – in boats. After this crossing, which caused many casualties (one of the special elephants was carried away by the torrential river), the army marched to Gwalior and then halted again at Narwar, a town near the elephant forests.

There the hunting began. Several hunting parties were formed which undertook to catch wild elephants with ropes, then drag them back to the camp and slowly tame them with grass, grain, water, and gentle persuasion. Akbar caught no fewer than nine elephants on this occasion and took such pleasure in the hunt that he prolonged it by many days. Mounting his horse at dawn, he spent these days traversing a forest where man had never set foot and which was described by Abu-l-Fazl as so dense that "the wind could not penetrate it." Here, to his delight (he thought it was a good omen), Akbar and his hunting party were able to find and catch a herd of another seventy elephants.

With these elephants safely tied to trees, Akbar decided it was time to turn his attention to administrative affairs. A royal assembly had to be organized in the midst of the jungle. Chamberlains and court carpenters were called upon to construct an improvised wooden platform and cover it with scarlet cloth for the royal repose. The courtiers took positions in a semi-circle around him. And thus the business of the Mughal government was conducted. During breaks there was time for the recital of stories for amusement.

So it went on until the time arrived for the real hunt to begin, or, as Abu-l-Fazl put it, "the hunt of yet another kind of wild elephants," by which he meant the rebel Abdullah Khan Uzbek and his companions. The expedition party continued toward Malwa. But progress was again slowed down by lightning, rain, and floods, vicious mud, as well as the numerous holes and ditches of the terrain. Elephants, horses, and camels had to swim across more rivers. Excessively heavy rains forced Akbar to pitch his camp for two days at the village of Ranad before being able to move on in the direction of Sarangpur. On this march there was so much mud at one point that the horses sank into it up to their chests and the hair of the camels became a burden to them. At another point a halt had to be called in order for tents which had fallen off and were about to be swept away by floods to be retrieved.

With a thousand more such difficulties, the imperial standards then moved in the direction of Mandu. A wide plain was reached, where the horses found plentiful fresh and moist grass, "skipping about with delight in verdant pastures." In Sarangpur, the first town of Malwa, Akbar received seven hundred fresh horses and mules from the governor and distributed them among his retinue. He then proceeded to Ujjain, the former capital of the kings of Malwa. Here he received the news that Abdullah Khan Uzbek, after some failed negotiations, had not repented but rather sent his family ahead while preparing to make a stand. In the engagement that followed, Abdullah Khan's party of more than one thousand horse was routed by Akbar and his three hundred followers. The air was thick and hot, but the pursuit of the rebel was resumed once again, at night and in heavy rains. Another engagement followed near Campanir. Here the rebel dishonorably abandoned all his women in the wilderness while making off with one of his sons toward Chingis Khan – the ruler in Gujarat. Akbar decided not to follow him there and halted his troops, gathering up the rebel's women, elephants, horses, and all the booty, and retreating, with these in tow, to Mandu, which he reached on August 10. Here he ordered a halt for one month to establish some order in the administration of the country and bring the local land-holders and magnates under his authority. From Mandu he dispatched "bulletins of victory" to Agra and all other parts of his imperial dominion. And he sent a request to Chingis Khan to deliver up the fugitive Uzbek rebel or expel him from Gujarat.

Akbar set out for Agra when, we read, the rainy season was at its very height. Again the march went through flooded plains. This time, amazing everyone, he mostly rode on the back of a mast[1] elephant he had chosen for its unequaled ferocity and obstinacy and which he kept under control with a special goad buried in the elephant's head. Traversing more mountains through storms and floods, the army reached Ujjain again, then Sarangpur, where a halt was ordered for one week, then Khirar, and Sipri. There the local forest tribe of Bhils brought the welcome news that a new herd of seventy elephants had been sighted in a nearby forest, including one mast elephant remarkable for the grace of its movements. Yet another hunt followed, at the end of which the whole herd, through ingenious means devised by Akbar, was driven into a fortress. Traveling back via Narwar and Gwalior, the same route as he had come, he arrived in Agra on October 9, almost three months after his departure.

He did not stay in the capital for long. That same year huntsmen brought more good news about herds of elephants roaming in the forests near Narwar. Again Akbar went hunting and wandered for two days in that endless forest before coming into the first herd. Abu-l-Fazl, at that point in his narrative, surmised that "a spectator might suppose that nothing but these amusements touched the hem of his [the emperor's] heart"(AN, II, 369). Early in the tenth year of his reign Akbar again went off for an elephant hunt in yet another nearby forest, this time in pursuit of a herd of 250 elephants. Only then was he compelled to give it up. "His Majesty's constitution," wrote Abu-l-Fazl, "became somewhat affected by the climate and long marches . . . in that warm, elephant-haunted country [which] was not conformable to the human constitution . . . [and] the hunting party fell ill, Akbar too" (AN, II, 370).

Akbar's long absences in the forests of Narwar, needless to say, had not remained unnoticed. During all this time, the revolt of the Uzbeks had been gaining momentum in Awadh under another of their leaders, Iskandar Khan. On May 24, 1565, Akbar therefore found himself involved in yet another campaign against his Uzbek rivals, crossing the Yamuna river with an army to face them in the east. Now the season was "excessively hot" and Akbar was forced to march only at night, stage by stage, until he reached Kanauj. From there he went on to the Ganges, which it took ten days to get the army across. Then, starting at midnight, Akbar went off on horseback to Lakhnau – where Iskandar Khan had shut himself up – riding continuously for one night and one day and again from dawn on a second day to surprise the rebel leader. Sikandar Khan barely escaped "half dead," but was still able to join two other leading Uzbek rebels, Bahadur Khan and Ali Quli, who, driving their families before them, had taken refuge on the other side of the Ganges. Akbar slowly made his way up to Jaunpur, in pursuit of these Uzbeks. He remained in the Awadh region for a long time, gradually gaining control of the rebellion by continuous and extensive campaigning, and he did not return to Agra again until March 28, 1566, almost ten months later.

EPISODE TWO: 1574

In the first episode Akbar was a young man between the ages of twenty-one and twenty-three, but it was not just in his youth that he was "roughing it," as the following two episodes will show.

The first is set in 1574, when Akbar was thirty-one, and he personally led a campaign against the Afghans of the eastern provinces (AN, III, 116–145). Again he left Agra at the beginning of the rainy season, but this time he traveled with the princes and a few of the ladies of the harem, as well as an entourage of courtiers. The royal party traveled together in large river boats, while the main army and the great camp traveled by land. The boats in which Akbar and his entourage were to travel had been especially designed and constructed for the occasion, under his personal directions. They were, wrote Abu-l-Fazl, beyond the powers of description: "There were various delightful quarters and decks, and there were gardens such as clever craftsmen could not make on land, on the boats. The sterns too, of every one of those water houses, were made in the shape of animals, so as to astonish spectators . . . There were wonderful instances of architecture, and various canopies and extraordinary decorations" (AN, III, 116). Two special elephants of extraordinary size were put on two separate boats, each with two female elephant companions. Altogether, it was an astonishing sight: "The numerous boats of various kinds, the hoisting of sky-high masts, the tumult of the waves of the river, the force of the wind, the rush of the clouds and the rain, the roar of the thunder, and the flashing of the lightning produced a strange appearance" (AN, III, 124). Akbar, from the first day of this expedition onward, left his boat every day to hunt deer with cheetahs, again (as in the previous episode) looking for omens in the results of the hunt and the behavior of animals for the success of the larger expedition.

At Etawah there was such a violent storm on the Yamuna river that many of the water houses were sunk by the waves. Of the ones that made it to the next halt, at Ilahabas (Allahabad), another eleven were sunk in a similar storm. The orchestra was damaged too, but saved by divine intervention. Near Chunar, after three days of rest and recreation at Varanasi, the river again became so boisterous that the naval authorities became alarmed and ordered most boats to be evacuated and their passengers to travel by land. Not Akbar, who went on by boat, cheerful and unperturbed, putting, as always, his faith in God – it appears that the boats reserved for his party were better built, and stormproof. At Cocakpur, the main army caught up with him and from then on started to pitch its tents opposite the stormproof royal barges.

When the main army was crossing the Karmnasa (a tributary of the Ganges which is regarded as ill-omened by Indians), more disasters were about to follow. First, one of the special elephants, of extraordinary size, was drowned. Then, a few days later, one of the boats carrying the hunting cheetahs was sunk, and the special cheetahs Dalat Khan and Dilrang were drowned in another storm. The world-conqueror, however, continued by river route in this season full of turbulence, and with constant rain and tempest, and reached his destination with a tranquil heart. His lieutenants in the east came out to welcome him and pay their respects, accompanied by boats loaded with various fireworks, gunners, and cannoneers for a good pyrotechnic display: "The noise, the smoke, and the concussion shook the earth, and the neighborhood for several parasangs became as dark as the fortunes of the enemies of dominion. The horrific noise wound its way into the brains of the darkened foe, and their gall-bladders became as water" (AN, III, 135).

EPISODE THREE: 1589

Akbar was not one to give up easily. We see this again in a third episode, in 1589, when he was in the thirty-fourth year of his reign and forty-seven years old. That was the year in which he finally realized his dream of visiting Kashmir, doing so, of course, against the advice of his courtiers (AN, III, 816–839).

He crossed the Ravi river in the Panjab. Three thousand stone cutters, mountain miners, and rock splitters were sent ahead together with two thousand diggers to level the road ahead of him. The route taken was to go through the Bhimbar pass, and it was known the passage was going to be difficult on account of the severe cold, and the heavy snow and rain, which bewildered the natives of India. For this reason the accompanying harem ladies were at first left behind at Bhimbar, at the bottom of the pass. Once he himself had passed through, and the road had been leveled, Akbar ordered his eldest son, Prince Salim, to go back and fetch the ladies.

But the prince returned without the ladies, reporting difficulties with the severe weather which forced him to leave them at Naushara. This would not do for Akbar. Standing in the midst of freezing rain between slippery ridges, he flew into a rage when he heard the report of his son and demanded his horse to be brought immediately so he could go and fetch them himself. The prince was so dejected he shut himself up in his tent and abandoned all food and sleep. Akbar, under pressure, gave up the idea of going back himself, and instead allowed the Khan Khanan to go. But he had his way. The entire caravan, including the large army, numerous elephants, and the harem, crossed into Kashmir successfully, and they all enjoyed the splendid spectacles and glorious air.

The difficulties of the journey notwithstanding, Akbar developed such a passion for the beauties and pleasures of Kashmir that he went back two more times. His second journey took place in 1592, again against all advice, and again, in spite of the clouds and the rain, and the mud, with several of his harem ladies accompanying him (AN, III, 943–959). An insurrection against the still relatively novel authority of the Mughal emperor had occurred in Kashmir just around that time. On July 22, when Akbar was about to go, the Kashmiris closed all the routes and passes into their country. Akbar was not deterred and forced them open, but this time he did have to leave his harem behind in Rohtas. Although he could not take them along he spent a month of that year's fall in the Kashmir valley. In 1597, in the forty-second year of his reign, when he was fifty-five years old, he went for a third time, with great and small trying to restrain him, and cut through the snow passes with an army and a following of such size that their presence seriously aggravated the already prevailing famine conditions in the "heavenly valley of Kashmir." This time he went fowling on Dal Lake – with his harem ladies.

TAMING THE MONGOL
BEASTS

As we saw in the previous chapter (p. 38), in Abu-l-Fazl's *Akbarnama* hunting and the taming of wild elephants and other beasts are an allegory for the taming of the Mongol nobles. This allegory depicting the Mongols as wild "beasts," recurrent in Abu-l-Fazl's writings, may well reflect negative perceptions of the pagan Mongol nomads or "Tartars" that had been current in medieval times.[2] Be that as it may, rather than dwell on their negative characteristics the main reason why Abu-l-Fazl expands on this subject is that in his time the descendants of the pagan Mongols who now ruled India were in the throes of a transformation of momentous consequences. It is the positive outcome of this transformation that concerns Abu-l-Fazl – because he regards it as one of Akbar's great achievements.

The "taming" or "civilizing" of the originally nomadic Mongols was, of course, a gradual process that took place over centuries. Under the Timurid princes, many Mongols had already attained a more sedentary, post-nomadic condition. The great transformation of Mongols into Mughals was well on its way when Akbar came to the throne. But it can be argued that it was completed by Akbar in the sixteenth century, and then taken to its highest levels by his successors on the Mughal throne.

This meant that a gap – ever-growing – opened up between the Mughals of India and the remaining nomadic and rude "Tartar" tribes that continued to roam the steppe lands stretching out to the Russian frontier. Many Uzbeks, in particular, having driven the Timurids from Bukhara, Khwarazm, and Ferghana in the fifteenth century, retained their nomadic lifestyle, breeding sheep, camels, and horses, throughout the sixteenth to eighteenth centuries, and well into the nineteenth century. This enduringly nomadic part of the Uzbek population also retained its reputation – which it shared with all nomadic "Tartars" (Mongols, Qalmuqs, and so on) – for ferocity and barbarism, producing swarms of light cavalry which were renowned for their predatory style of warfare and also for being astonishingly patient of hunger, thirst, and fatigue. Molded by the extremely harsh conditions of nomadic life in wild and desolate regions, they tended to be impetuous and violent even in the eighteenth and nineteenth centuries. They remained accustomed to sustaining life in enemy territory with the blood of their horses. Nineteenth-century accounts describe in vivid detail how, when they captured a sheep, camel, or horse on their plundering raids and could not carry it off, they would decapitate it and cut it up, putting the pieces between their saddle and the back of their horse to be eaten on the march whenever they were hungry. They killed everyone except Shi'is and infidels, whom they sold like cattle in Bukhara. Such descriptions of "Tartar" pastoral nomads in relatively recent times provide glimpses into the mode of life of the medieval Mongols. But they show a mode of life in retreat, one that has become anachronistic and marginalized. In effect, while pastoral nomadism survived into recent times, no great "Tartar" conquerors emerged from the steppes after the death of Timur in the early fifteenth century.

THE NEW COURT ETIQUETTE

Perhaps Akbar understood better than anyone else the necessity of taming the Mongol nobles. Such understanding may have come naturally to him as a consequence of the extreme insecurity of his own early years. If so, this may help explain Akbar's extraordinary emphasis on self-mastery and etiquette as a mode of political control.

For one thing, the old Mongol custom of informal fraternizing at frequent entertainments of commanders with soldiers, accompanied by excessive drinking (still common in Babur's time, as one can see in his autobiographical memoir, the *Baburnama*), was gradually abandoned. We know that Akbar was still attending such entertainments, at the mansions of his major nobles, very early in his reign, in and around 1558, but thereafter abandoned it. Around 1575, when the Timurid ruler of Badakhshan, Mirza Sulayman, came to Akbar's court for a visit, the old Mongol custom was revived in honor of the visitor and a banquet was arranged in the "customary" style. But when the Mirza left, the custom was abandoned again. Of course, Akbar continued to provide entertainments for noble visitors. No efforts were spared on these occasions, but they were not Mongol drinking bouts. He would also visit nobles at their expensively decorated homes. Even this we hear about only until 1582. Thereafter, both the visits and the accompanying entertainments, whether provided or received by him, practically ceased.

The abandonment of informal fraternizing went hand in hand with increasingly rigid court formalities. Barely into the fifth year of his reign, Akbar had one of his Mongol nobles arrested for saluting him from horseback. Ten or twelve years later, another Mongol noble who arrived drunk was removed from court and led around tied to a horse tail before being imprisoned. Abu-l-Fazl wrote that, by then, anyone who transgressed the code of etiquette of the eternal monarchy was verbally censured by the sovereign, as a lesson to all. Monserrate observed that by the 1580s the preservation of the emperor's dignity had become the major preoccupation of the court, even when on the move.

Abu-l-Fazl's *Ain-i-Akbari*, the great gazetteer of Akbar's reign, presents detailed regulations for admission to the court. It makes clear why these regulations were introduced at Akbar's command. It was because His Majesty looked upon the smallest details as "mirrors capable of reflecting the entire picture, and he does not ignore that which superficial observers call unimportant" (Ain, I, 165). Court etiquette went hand in hand with a new and thus far unknown discipline. As already alluded to, all of Akbar's nobles were given, apart from their titles, numerical ranks or "mansabs," and were thus formally fitted into a quantified status hierarchy which expressed uniformity, discipline, and cohesiveness and which was constantly reviewed and adjusted by the emperor himself.[3] Here the allegory of taming the Mongol "beasts" translates into an attempt to turn a loose, multi-ethnic and religiously heterogeneous assemblage of post-nomadic military retainers into a disciplined service nobility, while establishing a rigid court etiquette as a new force of counter-insurgency. This task was never easy, since Akbar — like any other ruler — could not afford to antagonize his nobles. It had to be done by a judicious mixture of force and persuasion — just like the taming of elephants, as Abu-l-Fazl says. It was less easy to the extent that alternative career paths were open to the nobles, as they were as long as Gujarat still existed as an independent Sultanate, and also during the short interval in which Akbar's half-brother Mirza Muhammad Hakim seemed to be emerging as a rival in the contest for loyalty in the Mughal dominion.

In later years, Akbar's court became like the court of Louis XIV — a system of etiquette as run by a drill sergeant. Akbar's philosophy was that the presence of the king should promote humility, since humility was the foundation of the moral order. With the view, then, to promote genuine humility, Akbar in his wisdom issued regulations prescribing prostration and new modes of salutation (one should bend down the head while keeping the palm of the right hand placed on the forehead). No one, except the royal princes, was to be allowed to remain seated in his presence, he declared. All present had to remain standing at their places, according to their rank, with their arms crossed. Enforced by his successors as "Akbar's rule," this could cause considerable embarrassment in the case of royal visitors. Manucci describes how Aurangzeb, not wishing to break "Akbar's rule," had to meet the king of Kashghar in a mosque, where being seated would be no dishonor, and where he could say "Salam Alaykum" ("Peace be upon you") as if to the angels (Manucci, III, 178).

Akbar's disciplinary zeal struck contemporaries as uncommon. "The King's severity towards errors and misdemeanors committed by officials in the course of government business is remarkable," wrote Monserrate, "and hence all are afraid of his severity, and strive with all their might to do as he directs and desires" (Monserrate, 209). The Mongol nobles were used to carrying arms from an early age and always remained proud and generally arrogant, even insolent; they were not people naturally inclined to unquestioning obedience. For all that, Akbar did in due course find ways of challenging their authority and bending them to his will. One of his more radical weapons was to assert his right to confiscate his nobles' accumulated wealth at their deaths, as he did from time to time. But his ultimate weapon was poison, an insidious device that he appears to have perfected and made routine, passing on the habit to his heirs. The way it worked was that Akbar would hide his irritation, no matter what the offence, thereby throwing off-guard any courtiers who were suspected of obstructing him. A confidential aide to the emperor would then administer poison to the cuffs and hood of a robe of honor that would be given to such suspected courtiers – it was a gift they could not refuse. Or Akbar gave the poison to them with his own hands, in a folded betel-leaf – another honor that could not be turned down in open court.

FROM CHINGIS KHAN TO AKBAR: THE RISE OF MUGHAL CIVILIZATION IN THE SIXTEENTH CENTURY

By the second half of the sixteenth century the emerging Mughal nobility was beginning to turn its back on the last remains of the legacy of its nomadic Mongol ancestors. Already fairly early in his reign (the seventh year) we get evidence that Akbar was cracking down on generals engaged in the still common Mongol practice, in times of war, of indiscriminately killing non-combatants, capturing women and children, and selling them as slaves. "It was the Code (Tora) of Chingis Khan," wrote Badauni, "to massacre or make slaves of all the inhabitants [of a conquered region] . . . to destroy utterly many towns and villages and sweep everything clean and clear . . . to value God's creation as if it were but radishes, cucumbers and leeks" (MT, II, 42–46). This old Mongol approach to warfare and conquest, while still followed by some of Akbar's generals in some parts of India in the early years of his reign, was not tolerated after the conquest of the Rajput fortress of Chitor in 1568, the one major occasion when Akbar himself still practiced the Chingisid "Code" and killed thousands of peasants along with their families, who were trapped in there.

Akbar also ordered that cultivated fields be guarded by orderlies so that they would not be trampled down by passing imperial troops (a practice which had also been enforced by Sher Shah), laying down that whatever damage was inflicted was to be compensated. At times by setting an example, at other times by regulation, or, when necessary, by the imposition of the severest military discipline, Akbar aimed to restrain all types of tyrannical behavior. He went on to discourage "excessive devotion to hunting," "incessant play," "drunkenness night and day," and "constant intercourse with women." Levity and anger, he insisted, had to be kept "under the restraint of reason."

It was still half a century and more before "the Mughal courts at Delhi and Agra had become schools of manners and good taste even for opponents and rebels" (Hardy, 17). In the 1580s, in the estimate of the Jesuit Rudolfo Acquaviva, the emperor "and all his men who are Mongols" still had "not a little of the barbarian" (Letters, 56). Ghastly torturing and dismemberment practices were still condoned, and the towers of skulls (and heads or dead bodies hung from trees) of vanquished opponents and rebellious peasants along the imperial highway from Agra to Delhi remained a potent reminder to all its users of the "barbarian" origins of India's newest ruling class. Even as the seventeenth century advanced, some of these practices (which were introduced into India by Akbar) remained in vogue, forcing travelers on these roads to hold their noses on account of the odor from the dead. After his own death, Akbar's grave was vandalized, his bones allegedly scattered, by peasants who had once suffered such treatment and could only think of exacting vengeance from him posthumously. Nonetheless, the "Code of Chingis Khan" had mostly been rendered innocuous by that time, surviving mainly in matters of protocol.

Instead, a distinctive sense of cultural superiority that had been growing at the Timurid courts in Samarqand, Heart, and Kabul, re-emerged and grew under Akbar in the second half of the sixteenth century, to become unshakeable under his successors. It was a sense of separate identity that manifested itself in the increasingly dismissive attitude of the Mughals toward their still nomadic or semi-nomadic neighbors, such as the Uzbeks, and indeed toward their own nomadic ancestors. It also manifested itself in their view of the "rustic"Afghans of Roh (in eastern Afghanistan), whom the Mughals distinguished from the Indo-Afghans by their complete lack of "delicate breeding and graceful accomplishments," and, in effect, of the tribal populations of India and neighboring territories generally. Jahangir, observing the Magh tribes of Pegu and Arakan (in modern Myanmar), wrote in his autobiography: "Briefly they are beasts in the form of men. They eat everything there is on land or in the sea, and nothing is forbidden by their religion. They eat with everyone : . . . They have no proper religion . . . They are far from the Muslim faith and separated from that of the Hindus" (Tuzuk, I, 236). Akbar's eldest son and successor generally contrasted the "ways of the men of the wilds" with "civilized ways." In less than a century, a new Mughal self-consciousness had thus given rise to a remarkable reversal of perspective. "Civilized ways" were now identified with the ways of the Mughal court.

MAXIMS OF ORDER

Akbar's disciplinary drive and niggling attention to detail are most in evidence in the realm of revenue collection and administration, and in his bureaucratic regulations (which were themselves a form of etiquette). Here we encounter the real fulcrum of his attempt at taming the Mongol "beasts," of his "civilizing mission." Here too Akbar had forerunners, but they appear to have been much less emphatic and bold. As early as the 1540s, the Afghan ruler Sher Shah cracked down on the aristocratic prejudice against bothering with the petty details of daily administration, which the grandees would dismiss as the domain of lowly shopkeepers. Akbar, like Sher Shah, subscribed to the idea that truly great kings did not confine their attention to great things, and promoted himself as a friend of good order and propriety in administrative business, no matter how small.

Before Sher Shah and Akbar's time, the collection and expenditure of revenue had been a haphazard operation. The medieval Mongol khans had conquered and commanded, or killed, but they had not felt much inclination to keep records or submit reports for auditing. Akbar, however, insisted that a radically scientific survey of the country's resources and products of all kinds be made, based on standardized measures and uniform criteria. Throughout his life he would demand exact information along with receipts, not shunning to do ignoble paperwork himself. There was of course much more of it than he could manage, so he set up specialized daftars or "offices" of records which enabled him to conduct audits and formulate and constantly adjust guidelines for future action.

Just as in early modern Europe the increased demands for conscientious bureaucrats helped to turn the bourgeoisie into the main agency of monarchical rule, in sixteenth-century Mughal India the same demands brought the Hindu banking and financier castes to power and prominence – notably the caste of the Khatris, of whom Akbar's finance minister Raja Todar Mal was the most illustrious representative (he had honed his talents under Sher Shah). And just as early modern Europe saw the decline of chivalry and the social demotion of the knight, so Mughal India saw the decline, and ultimately the demise, of the "Code of Chingis Khan." Like Colbert in France, Todar Mal, charged with far-reaching revenue reforms, devised "maxims of order" to replace "maxims of confusion" and put in place a growing number of agents who developed Akbar's conception of the state as a business enterprise.

Mughal administration had to be made efficient and profitable; corruption had to be stamped out. The taming of the nobles was to be achieved not just by the imposition of a new court etiquette, or by putting them in the strait-jacket of the system of quantified ranks or "mansabs," but also by the introduction of revenue settlements, administrative regulations, and a never-ending series of revisions of these. Not a year passed without "good institutions" being devised. Facilitated by the new inflow of precious metals from the conquered territories and from the New World, Africa, and Japan, above all through Portuguese trade in Gujarat, prodigious quantities of coin were minted under Akbar which encouraged all parties to support the conversion of agricultural produce into money, thereby further corroding primordial service relationships at all levels, and enhancing accountability.

The results were limited, but they were nonetheless real, and they made Akbar an emperor with a reputation for frugality as much as for his extraordinary wealth. As Monserrate put it, "Zelaldinus [Jalal ad-Din, i.e. Akbar] is sparing and tenacious of his wealth, and thus has become the richest Oriental king for at least 200 years" (Monserrate, 208). Akbar, by promoting government by inquiry, was an emperor who sponsored the Hindu banking and financier castes and the bourgeois virtues that they exemplified – of which frugality is one. For their part, the nobles were, needless to say, reluctant to submit to this fiscal discipline. Many found the new regulations oppressive and menacing, and they were worried about being crushed under Todar Mal's juggernaut. For Abu-l-Fazl, however, this was one of the foundations of Akbar's success. It had the sanctity of religion: "By wise regulations the revenue was preserved, which is the highest form of worship in the state" (AN, III, 341). Abu-l-Fazl also wrote: "True greatness, in spiritual and worldly matters, does not shrink from the minutiae of business, but regards their performance as an act of divine worship" (Ain, I, 11). Another contemporary historian of Akbar's reign, al-Qandahari, goes even further. "To establish good administration and organization," he wrote, "is higher than the ability to perform one's religious duties"(TAK, 20).

The new demands were followed by a demand for clear naming and a "sharpening of identification" which was also characteristic of early modern Europe (Barzun, 115). "When His Majesty had fixed the ranks of the army, and inquired into the quality of the horses," continues Abu-l-Fazl, "he ordered that upright scribes should make out descriptive rolls of the soldiers and write down their peculiar marks. Their ages, the names of their fathers, dwelling-places, and race were to be registered . . . Everyone who wished to join the army was taken before His Majesty, in whose presence his rank was fixed" (Ain, I, 265). A trace of this office may have existed in earlier times, but "its higher objects were but recognized in the present reign" (Ain, I, 268). The true excellence of keeping records had been recognized by the illiterate emperor Akbar. It was he who demanded that everything had to be recorded, including the orders and the doings of His Majesty himself and whatever the heads of departments reported, whatever His Majesty ate and drank, when he slept, when he rose, the time he spent in the harem, what books he had read out to him, his fasts, his appointments to mansabs, his victories, his card games, the rules of etiquette he enforced in the state hall, the tallies of beasts killed in the royal hunts – indeed everything.

HUNTING AND GOVERNMENT

Even the royal hunt, the aristocratic leisure activity par excellence, had to be recast as a governmental duty pure and simple, or so at least at the level of Abu-l-Fazl's rhetoric. Conceiving of hunting as a form of control, Abu-l-Fazl reduced it entirely to a purposeful governing and military activity, and even to a form of "communication with God," in an emphatic attempt to strip it of all its aristocratic, conspicuous-leisure, and at times even frivolous connotations. No longer an indulgence, hunting too became, as Abu-l-Fazl saw it, a religious and spiritual task.

To be sure, the royal hunt had never been solely a matter of pleasure to the ruling elites of Asia. While it did not have much of an economic role (since providing something to eat for the hunter had never been its main purpose), it had long been a tool of government, of diplomacy, or reconnaissance (as the "shooting leave" still was in the days of the Great Game), and also a training opportunity for war. At a time when there were still vast tracts of forests everywhere, it was also an opportunity to display royal prowess by mobilizing magnificent hunting parties on a grand scale and far afield (which by itself could in some cases make war unnecessary). All this was especially true for the spectacular Mongol "ring hunt" or *qamargha*, which involved thousands of hunters and a tally, not uncommonly, of tens of thousands of dead animals.

Akbar, throughout his life, hunted a great deal in all sorts of ways. As our texts say, "he was always disposed to traveling and hunting," with thousands of accompanying huntsmen and beaters (and not uncommonly with his harem ladies as well), more, probably much more, than any other Mughal emperor ever was. He was especially fond of elephant hunting, and – from early boyhood – of hunting with cheetahs (he owned a thousand and regarded them as "one of God's wonders"). He knew the names of all the thousands of other beasts kept at his court, horses, asses, deer, elephants, and cheetahs alike; and some beasts, magnificently dressed and bejeweled, obtained official ranks for especially heroic performances.

But, as it is presented in Abu-l-Fazl's *Akbarnama*, for Akbar the royal hunt acquired a new meaning. Abu-l-Fazl gives it a religious purposefulness, casting it as a routine of discipline pleasing to God, and repeatedly denying that Akbar was wasting his time in the unnecessary pursuit of pleasure or that he was trying to evade his governmental obligations when he went hunting. On the contrary, as Abu-l-Fazl presented it, when Akbar was hunting big game he was in reality governing, only more so – because hunting was an expedient for the control of beasts and nobles alike. When Akbar was hunting it seemed he was indifferent to state affairs, but in reality this was not so. He was testing men. When hunting in appearance he was inwardly with God and engaged in the capture of souls. Indeed, when he placed thousands of deer antlers along the imperial road from Agra to Ajmer, he was demonstrating his power over beasts as effectively as he did when taming mast elephants, Abu-l-Fazl says, emphasizing that Akbar rode more than a hundred times on mast elephants which had killed their drivers.

MONGOL VEGETARIANS

It was when hunting that Akbar had some of his most important religious insights. In one case, occurring in 1578, it induced him to liberate all the animals in the hunting ring – a course of action that caused such confusion about the emperor's state of mind that it led to political disturbances in the eastern provinces and prompted a visit by his mother. On this occasion startled observers noted how the emperor's vision became brilliant, how a sublime joy took hold of his bodily frame, and how he entered a trance – the hunting ground was later declared a "mini-Mecca." Some thought he had met a holy spirit there, or that the silent ones of the wilderness had given him a message. Others thought the beasts of the forests had imparted divine secrets to him. Paradoxically, the experience made Akbar decide to try becoming a vegetarian.

He was not the first Mongol to try. Nor the last. His father Humayun is on record as having given up meat temporarily at the time he re-conquered Delhi. His son Jahangir observed a vow not to kill animals for four years (1618–1622) and on certain days ate vegetarian food out of respect for his father. There are other examples in Indian history of kings who experienced a hunting nausea and then gave up hunting and began to abstain from most meats as a source of nutrition, including the famous Buddhist king Ashoka. But for Akbar the pursuit of vegetarianism became an obsession, even though he never gave up hunting. What is more, he also introduced vegetarianism to the Mughal nobility, in a cautious and gradual way, but not without success – if we can rely on Abu-l-Fazl's information. In this he went beyond attempts (which were also common) to restrain beef consumption which catered specifically to Hindu religious beliefs regarding the sacredness of cows. To his nobles he invoked the beauty of preventing cruelty. Here again Abu-l-Fazl resorts to the allegory of taming wild beasts: "Inasmuch as he was aware of the wolfish nature of men he considered that to tame them all at once would be to distress and pain the votaries of custom. Therefore the inspiration came to his holy heart that he would stretch out his hand slowly and by degrees so that things might not be difficult for the followers of truth, and that general apprehensions might not drive them crazy" (AN, III, 332). Since Akbar himself never quite achieved his goal he cannot have been a perfect role model for his nobles. He sometimes abstained from meat on certain days only (Fridays, the eighteenth of each solar month, the first of each solar month, days he was already fasting, days between fasts, days of solar eclipses, days of lunar eclipses, his birthday, his accession day, and so on), or for some months at a time (nine months in one year was the maximum), as a religious penance – just as he gave up garlic and onions on certain days, or suspended, but never gave up, hunting. In the end, although he said he had never really cared for meat since his earliest years and found it rather tasteless, preferring "Sufi food," he did not always go much beyond meat-free (and meat-that-he-had-killed-himself-free) days. It was his aim, however, eventually to discontinue meat entirely. At some point he began to regard himself as a "social carnivore." "If the scarf of social life were not on my shoulder, I would restrain myself from eating meat," he recorded in 1578 (AN, III, 332). Exactly how many nobles at his court continued to practice vegetarianism is unfortunately not known. If Abu-l-Fazl can be relied on, however, it did spread among the nobles to an extent that was remarkable.

By the standards of both the time and his elevated social position, Akbar was a very moderate consumer of alcohol and other intoxicants. Historians have often dwelt on the high proportion of medieval Mongol nobles who died young from excessive indulgence in the staple alcoholic drink of the steppe, *qumis*, fermented horse milk. Akbar's hard-drinking (alcoholic?) ancestors Babur and Humayun switched from *qumis* to wine (the fine wines from Kafiristan and Bajaur were brought to them by "mule loads" and "boatloads") and to distilled and double-distilled spirits (arrak), but they represented the same centuries-old tradition of the steppes. For them there was also opium, or *ma'jun* — a drug made from an extract of plums, apricots, and certain other fruits, mixed with opium, still known today. Because of its easy portability, opium (or ma'jun) was often preferred on military campaigns. In the kingdom of Kabul, when Akbar was growing up, military campaigns were entirely dependent on the availability of opium. If the poppy harvest failed, it meant the end of a season's campaigning. Whenever opium and poppy-heads became excessively expensive, no Afghan warlord would advance further. The Yusufzai tribesmen of the plains carried this type of intoxication to the utmost excess. So did the Rajput warriors of India. It was interesting to see them, wrote François Bernier (a French doctor), on the eve of battle, "with the fumes of opium in their heads," rushing into the thick of combat insensible to danger. In areas close to the production grounds, opium was consumed in amazingly high doses in the battle mêlée, by warriors, horses, and elephants alike — making a clean sweep of the entire supply that had not already been diverted into various more domestic applications in smaller doses.

As with meat, Akbar did not entirely abstain from the consumption of opium, wine, or spirits either (although he appears to have left *qumis* behind without too many regrets), but he was a moderate user and seems to have been abstemious for considerable periods. In his public policy Akbar did not just pursue moderation but went so far as to issue prohibitions of both alcohol (from which only Europeans and medical users were exempted) and opium. Al-Qandahari wrote about Akbar: "He is such a paragon of justice that he has purified the whole country from the dirt and sin of drinking and fornication. In spite of the fact that the state gets a very substantial revenue from the public shops (drinking houses) serving light drinks, brothels, and gambling dens, he sacrificed this income once and for all" (TAK, 55). And: "Indulging in intoxicants and being reckless is not a worthy habit of emperors. It is best for them to be always awake and watchful . . . He [Akbar] is the king who escaped wine in obedience to God's command" (TAK, 172–173). Other historians of the time, including Badauni, confirm that Akbar laid down severe punishments

for excessive drinking and disorderly conduct, adding that prostitutes were banned to the suburbs of "Shaitanpura" ("Satan's town"),
and could no longer be taken home. Of course, in the end the ban on
drinking failed miserably (as probably the ban on prostitutes did
too): two of Akbar's sons died in their early thirties in an advanced
state of delirium tremens, and the third son, Jahangir, was a lifelong
addict of wine, arrak ("secreto"), and opium (not necessarily in that
order). But, for some time at least, Akbar's example seems to
have set a pattern of moderation and abstemiousness among the
Mongol nobles. We read that it was through Jahangir's example that
drinking became customary again, at court, and even in the harems.
Wines and distillates from Persia, Kabul, and Kashmir were smug-
gled into the royal harem in Shah Jahan's time. By then we find
mullas agitating for prohibitions of women drinking "wines from
Shiraz," and eating bhang (dried hemp leaves, normally left to the
poor), nutmeg, opium, and other drugs. Manucci, who, as a doctor,
had privileged access to the royal harem in the later seventeenth century, observed: "They [the guards] search everything with great care
to stop the entry of bhang, wine, ophion, nutmeg, or other drugs
which could intoxicate, for all women in mahals [the harem quarters]
love much such beverages. Nor do they permit the entry into the
palace of radishes, cucumbers, or similar vegetables that I cannot
name [not naming them was, for Manucci, a way of drawing attention
to the fact that they were used as sexual stimulants]" (Manucci, III,
328). Akbar himself, however, according to contemporary Jesuit
accounts, "rarely" drank wine. The same is true of the ladies of his
harem – if negative evidence can be any guide. Akbar did, on the
other hand, drink the water known as *post*, an opium mixture
(also known as *koknar*) that made him fall asleep during discussions
with the Jesuits, and which gave him constipation. "When he has
drunk immoderately of *post*," wrote Monserrate, "he sinks back
stupefied and shaking" (Monserrate, 199). It was the same drink that
Aurangzeb later offered his captive brothers in Gwalior. Taking
away all appetite for food, it could be counted on to deliver a slow
but secret death.

The *Ain-i-Akbari* does not list tobacco among the crops cultivated in the Mughal empire of Akbar's time, suggesting that it was not grown there yet. But we do not lack a description of how tobacco was first presented to Akbar, close to the end of his life, by a courtier who brought it from Bijapur and Aceh (North Sumatra). Akbar, it may be concluded from this description, approached tobacco with his usual openness to experimentation and new discoveries, almost in a scientific spirit, rejecting out of hand his physician's claim that it must be bad for him. The aging emperor took some puffs from a pipe (we do not learn if he inhaled), and then gave it back. It would have been a bit late in the day for Akbar to start smoking, but in any case we know he did not. Some of his nobles immediately did, however; and soon afterwards, by the mid-seventeenth century at the latest, smoking tobacco was becoming very widespread in India, even among children as young as three and four years old. This originally New World crop rapidly came to be grown everywhere. Attempts to curtail smoking were not lacking, if not under Akbar, definitely under his (otherwise addicted) son and successor Jahangir, who ordered that no one should smoke tobacco because it was bad for one's health. Shah Abbas of Iran ordered a general prohibition of tobacco at about the same time, for the same reason.

THE EMPEROR NEVER WASTES HIS TIME

Even though Monserrate describes Akbar as a person "of a somewhat morose disposition," there is no indication that he turned against the enjoyment of life and all it had to offer in the way the German sociologist Max Weber held to be typical of the Puritans of early modern Europe (Monserrate, 197). On the other hand, many of Akbar's imperial regulations do remind us of the new attitudes to religious, social, economic, and political organization that emerged in Europe during the Reformation era.

These imperial regulations served a different purpose – owing to the fact that Akbar's situation was quite different from that of the sixteenth-century townspeople of northwestern Europe. The latter developed their worldly asceticism in response to the indulgences of the Catholic church and concomitant with the development of a new business ethics that served capital accumulation. Akbar was, above all, preoccupied with the problem of establishing imperial authority and how to extend it.

For Akbar the tools of bureaucracy, record keeping, information gathering ("daily journals of events obtained from all cities and towns"), as also the enforcement of court etiquette, and of moderation in everything, were primarily geared to the necessity of taming his post-nomadic conquest nobility. His demand for methodical work habits, rational self-control, and the efficient management of time (which in Reformation Europe culminated in the idea that "time is money") was dictated by the same imperial agenda.

Abu-l-Fazl summarizes Akbar's broader aim in 1573 as follows: "The sovereign aims to enable the inhabitants of every country . . . to establish harmony between their outward and inward condition . . . [to abandon self-exaltation and] . . . to become disciplined, so that while not deserving the appellation of ignorant they may also not merit the description of being idle and foolish" (AN, III, 96). He goes on to explain how before Akbar's reign the servants of the threshold paid no attention to time and season but lingered around the court continually, while the rest of the people were lethargic and slothful. But when Akbar came to the throne the slothful were guided to activity, and fresh luster was brought to court, things were "knit together," and the opportunity of service fell into the hands of the energetic while the slothful became depressed. Everything in the palace came to be regulated by a water clock. At fixed hours the time was struck on bronze gongs, and bells were rung, drums beaten, and trumpets sounded at fixed intervals.

Then, in the recordings of 1578 – the year in which he released the animals caught in a ring hunt – we read that Akbar began to "watch over his being" and "cherish his time," and that from then onward he no longer spent any portion of it idly. From this year onward he began to divide the days and nights in fixed portions, each earmarked for a specific activity, "for the guidance of the fortunate," and "to set an example for mankind." There was time set apart for devotion after arising from sleep, time to give attention to the body, clothing, and toilet, time for food, time to be spent attending the elephants, horses, camels, and mules, time to be spent in the female apartments, time for napping, and so on. For this, as for almost every other measure that Akbar introduced, there were antecedents. Sulayman Kararani, the Afghan ruler of Bengal, had a schedule for everything, one from which he never deviated. Sultan Sikandar Lodi remained wide awake at night, slept during midday, and reserved for every task an appointed time that was never changed; even his conversation was strictly disciplined, and never desultory. Sher Shah was reportedly also occupied with the business of his kingdom around the clock, dividing each day and night into fixed portions for separate administrative and other tasks, never suffering idleness or sloth. Akbar had apparently heard how these contemporary Afghan rulers managed their time, imposing an iron discipline on themselves. The basic idea was not new. Akbar, however, became obsessed with time, experimenting with schedules and revised schedules for the hours of the day, days of the week, and months of the year throughout his later life, and especially when he was on tour. As in the case of "meatless days" he never decided on any single fixed schedule. Rather, Akbar's spiritual drive for discipline went into overdrive.

The vast compendium of Akbarian rules and regulations compiled by Abu-l-Fazl and known as the *Ain-i-Akbari* abundantly testifies to that. This work – which is distinctive of Akbar's and no other reign – is more than just an imperial gazetteer or a template of a new political order. Akbar is here depicted as if he were Gulliver – Jonathan Swift's fictional character who looked at his watch so often that his hosts the Brobdingnagians thought he was consulting his God. The *Ain-i-Akbari* is the product of an obsession with order which demanded everything to be recorded, nothing to be left to chance, no mistakes to be made, nothing to remain for messy discussion, no time to be wasted, and which, in a nutshell, did not fall short of an imagined universe of duties and obligations universally recognized by people – foremost Akbar himself – whose beastly impulses were finally and utterly tamed. It was a spiritual triumph of sorts, complementary to the military one:

> The care with which His Majesty guards over his motives, and watches over his emotions, bears on its face the sign of the infinite, and the stamp of immortality; and although thousands of important matters occupy, at one and the same time, his attention, they do not stir up the rubbish of confusion in the temple of his mind, nor do they allow the dust of dismay to settle on the vigor of his mental powers, or the habitual earnestness with which His Majesty contemplates the charms of God's world . . . Knowing the value of a lifetime, he never wastes his time, nor does he omit any necessary duty, so that in the light of his upright intentions, every action of his life may be considered as an adoration of God . . . He passes every moment of his life in self-examination or in adoration of God . . . in the morning, at noon . . . in the evening . . . [and] at midnight.
>
> [Ain, I, 162–163]

Akbar was supposedly an emperor who almost never slept. "He takes little repose in the evening, and again a short time in the morning; but his sleep looks more like waking . . . His Majesty is accustomed to spending the hours of the night profitably" (Ain, I, 164). Among Akbar's sayings recorded in the *Ain-i-Akbari* we read: "Worldlings should lead a busy life in order that idleness may be discouraged and that desires do not wander towards unlawful objects" (Ain, I, 429) and: "Idleness is the root of evil" (Ain, I, 450).

We do not have to accept all of this as an accurate depiction of Akbar's real-life conduct. Yet it is striking that the picture of Akbar presented by Abu-l-Fazl is not so very different from what the Jesuit Francis Henriques observed: "His preoccupations . . . are many and are very weighty, since almost everything must be routed through him, which is quite a lot, and this [is done] with great calmness and tranquillity, without any sign of disquiet . . . He is very hard-working; to this end he is never idle" (Letters, 21–22).

6

MAKER OF THE
INDO-MUSLIM WORLD

Historians agree that Akbar was the chief architect of all major Mughal institutions. As a recent work informs us, "The key to understanding the Mughal polity lies . . . in the first half of Akbar's reign . . . The first half of Akbar's reign saw the development of a new set of administrative institutions and practices, a new conception of kingship and the constitution of government and society, a new military system, and new norms of political behavior" (Streusand, 2, 14). Or again, "The Mughal polity, so long as it functioned with any effectiveness, say, until the early years of the eighteenth century, continued basically with the organizational forms that Akbar instituted" (Athar Ali, xi). Many have concluded that this is the reason why Akbar should be seen as the real founder of the Mughal empire. Some have gone so far as to suggest that Akbar had a "genius for organization" (Smith, 354).

Such a consensus among historians is deceptive. For the exact nature of all Mughal institutions created by Akbar has been the subject of at least some controversy, and sometimes has given rise to different, or even irreconcilable, interpretations. How centralized was the empire he founded? What caused its decline in the eighteenth century? These questions are still being debated. In addition, the value of the *Ain-i-Akbari* for the understanding of the Mughal empire and its operations has been a subject of disagreement. While some have regarded its detailed land surveys, production figures, price indices, and other statistics as unproblematic and as evidence of an immensely powerful and centralized bureaucratic organization, others have regarded them as suspect and even useless, if for no other reason than that they sometimes appear to contradict themselves. Again others have pointed out that the Mughal empire did not have the ethic, institutions, and recruitment procedures of a centralized bureaucracy but operated at best with the self-selecting agencies of a "patrimonial" or "household" bureaucracy. Or that the Mughal regime's Indian foundations ruled out such untrammeled centralized power as sometimes seems to be imputed to it in the *Ain-i-Akbari*. There is the further problem that the original revenue records of Akbar's time are no longer extant and that the sources from which Abu-l-Fazl drew his information are never acknowledged. The question has also been asked: for whose eyes were these figures and statistics intended? There is no answer to this question yet.

The basic idea that Akbar was a great institution builder, however, has never been questioned, and for good reason. Akbar clearly was the architect of Mughal India. There is perhaps only one other general characteristic of Akbar's reign that contemporary historians are equally unanimous about, namely that Akbar, for all his "genius for organization," invented virtually nothing that was completely novel in his time but in fact elaborated, systematized, reformed, or transformed an institutional heritage that was passed on to him by either the immediate or the medieval predecessors of the Mughals. In addition to a very large part of the physical infrastructure of fortresses, roads, and *sarais* or "travelers' lodges," the principles of bureaucratic and military organization, the "ranking" (mansab) system of the nobility, and even the currency system with the silver "rupees" that Akbar developed can all be traced back not to Babur and Humayun but to Sher Shah and the Afghan Suri empire, the medieval Indo-Islamic governments of the sultanate of Delhi and its successors, or to the Turko-Mongol steppe tradition represented by his ancestors Chingis Khan and Timur. Almost the entirety of this institutional legacy remained intact, albeit with modifications, under his successors

Jahangir (r. 1605–1627), Shah Jahan (r. 1627–1658), and Aurangzeb (r. 1658–1707); some of it even survived up to the reign of Muhammad Shah (r. 1719–1748) and was adopted by so-called Mughal "successor states" of the eighteenth century, such as the Marathas of the Deccan and the British East India Company in Bengal.

GUNPOWDER EMPIRES

Favorable circumstances and "genius for organization" aside, why was Akbar successful in building administrative institutions in India that continued to function and expand for well over a century and a half when his medieval predecessors had failed to do so? One, now partly outdated, explanation has been that a technological innovation, the introduction of artillery and other gunpowder weapons, was the decisive factor. This seemed plausible since the introduction of similar military technology had, according to a general understanding, made possible the phenomenal expansion of Portuguese naval power in the Indian Ocean in the same century. As we have seen in Chapter 3, there was intense competition for artillery between the major states of the time, and the Mughal army under Akbar enjoyed a virtual monopoly of artillery over its Indian opponents. After the conquest of Gujarat, Mughal control of Ottoman artillery supplies was complete, and ever afterwards artillery remained an important asset of the Mughal armies wherever they went.

The Russian orientalist Vasilii Bartold (1966), followed by world historians Marshall G. S. Hodgson (1974) and William H. McNeill (1982), first asserted that the diffusion of gunpowder weapons, in particular siege artillery, amounted to a "military revolution" and that this largely explains the increase and consolidation of central power in the three great sixteenth-century Muslim empires of the Ottomans, Safawids, and Mughals. For them, these were the "gunpowder empires" of the early modern Islamic world. In Hodgson's view, siege and field artillery provided a decisive advantage: "The

implications of the changes in weapons were not restricted entirely
to military organization. The relative expensiveness of artillery and
the relative untenability of stone fortresses gave an increased advantage over local military garrisons to a well-organized central power
which could afford artillery . . . Gunpowder was doubtless not the
one great decisive factor in the political and social – and ultimately
cultural – realignments that occurred in the three generations following 1450; but it played a distinctive role, and perhaps was the
most easily identifiable single occasion for them" (Hodgson, III,
17–18). In Europe too the diffusion of effective siege artillery had
made stone fortresses "untenable" – as was first demonstrated during
the French invasion of Italy in 1494. In Europe, however, the situation was reversed within a matter of decades with the development
of a new type of stone bastion, the *trace italienne*, which was an effective response against siege artillery. No such new developments in
fortification took off in the Muslim world and here, the argument
runs, artillery remained an advantage for those centralizing powers
which "could afford to be abreast of the latest improvements"
(Hodgson, III, 18).

As it was originally formulated in this way, the "gunpowder
empires" thesis is no longer convincing. A growing number of critics
has contended that, while it is true that there were no technical
improvements in fortification in India in the sixteenth and seventeenth centuries and that these, in effect, continued to resemble
medieval European castles, this is because Mughal artillery, while
carried along with the moving camps, was not an important element
of siege craft (Duffy, 9–13; Streusand, 12–13, 66–68; Gommans,
133–136). Most of the fortresses of Hindustan were located at sites
that could not be reached by guns, or only with the greatest difficulty.
If such strong hill fortresses as Chitor, Ranthambor, or Asirgarh were
successfully besieged and taken by Mughal armies, it was not due to
their use of artillery in breaching the stone walls. Fortresses, when
taken, were not destroyed either; quite the opposite, more fortresses
were built by Akbar and later Mughal emperors on essentially the
same pattern. In Mughal hands, they became the seats of provincial

governors, obstacles to rather than centers of revolt. Fortresses, cavalry, infantry, and artillery – all were important factors in maintaining Mughal military superiority, but artillery was not often the main and certainly never the only impetus toward centralization. It merely was one contributing factor among others and only for as long as the imperial center could maintain a monopoly on it. In later times it could also undermine the central authority of the Mughals when regional Hindu forces became equipped with artillery as well. Toned down in this way, the thesis still has some validity. But it is misleading to call the Mughal empire as it evolved under Akbar a "gunpowder empire" since cavalry, not artillery, remained its chief military asset.

AMERICAN SILVER

Another and more adequate explanation for the success of Akbar's institution building is derived from the availability of vast amounts of precious metals, in particular silver from the newly discovered Americas, for minting purposes throughout the expanding empire. The dramatically enhanced circulation of money, it is rightly argued, was a crucial factor that changed the conditions for deployment of power. The new money economy or "cash nexus" of the later sixteenth century drove fiscal reform and the establishment of a more effective bureaucracy. More fundamentally, it introduced a pronounced monetary dimension to political relations, corroding older forms of political loyalty based on ethnic, clan, or religious ties, and turned the political process into "political arithmetic."

Thanks to the study of numismatics we can, in effect, trace the beginnings of the remarkable Mughal monetary system to Akbar's reign. Surviving coins – especially the silver "rupees" of eleven grams – indicate that uniformly high standards were maintained from the early reign of Akbar until the break-up of the empire in the first half of the eighteenth century. They show that, as the empire expanded, the area of the circulation of the rupee, as well as its copper and gold counterparts, increased with it, superseding local and regional currencies of older dates. Most striking is the sheer volume of such coins. The number of rupees and copper coins issued by Mughal mints far exceeded that of any previous Indo-Muslim or Hindu regime and must have run in the tens of millions.

Since the domestic production of the Indian subcontinent was almost negligible (very small amounts of gold were obtained from alluvial river washing in the northern mountains and hills, and silver from some mines in Rajasthan), Akbar could obtain new supplies of precious metals only by appropriating the treasures of vanquished rulers or through import. The first of these sources was non-renewable. The second source – import – had no such limitation but, to the contrary, gained enormously in importance during Akbar's reign, especially after the conquest of Gujarat brought Portuguese trade within the Mughal orbit.

Precious metals had reached India through both maritime and overland routes from ancient times, from the west as well as from the east. Owing to the inherent strength of its economy, the Indian subcontinent had always enjoyed a favorable commodity balance of trade. Indian products, like spices and textiles and an almost infinite array of others, were in such great demand that the subcontinent was an importer of precious metals – a "sponge" country soaking up precious metals from all over the old world. Its imports were not counterbalanced by a drain of coin exports. In the medieval (seventh to fifteenth) centuries, gold and silver entered India from various parts of Africa, from Southeast Asia, as well as from Central Asia. But these supplies were hardly adequate to meet demand, and, as a consequence, there had been a silver famine in late medieval times.

When in Akbar's reign a flood of precious metals began pouring in through the new Iberian connections with the Americas (and Japan), the medieval silver famine that had hampered the institution-building efforts of his predecessors came to an end in a matter of decades. In addition to the precious metals they obtained through conquest and dehoarding, the Mughals relied heavily on these imports, and decade after decade this source allowed them, through a system of "free" minting open to all, to put more and more imperial coin into circulation, thus providing for themselves the monetary underpinnings of an economy that remained in step with emerging global markets.

Like all of Akbar's institutions, the currency system was the product of a long and halting evolution. What circulated in northern India between 1540 and 1556 was the coinage struck by the Afghan ruler Sher Shah Suri and his successors. This consisted of the silver rupee and copper paisa, both coins of an Indian type and resembling earlier currencies of the medieval Indo-Muslim states. The Mughals brought from Central Asia the silver "shahrukhi," a coin with a distinctive Timurid and Uzbek calligraphic style which had originally been confined to areas north of the Hindu Kush but which became the accepted currency in Kabul under Babur and Humayun and was also introduced in a few mints in Hindustan during the wars of reconquest. But the "shahrukhi" system never became widely accepted in Hindustan, and soon its mintage was discontinued. In his attempt to foster a strong currency Akbar then chose to perpetuate the monetary system of his Afghan-Suri predecessors rather than that of his own ancestors. This led to a massive re-coinage of Afghan-Suri currency, and, from 1564 onward, the production of an additional gold coinage – the *muhr* – which had been unknown to the Suris. As a result, by 1577, there was a "new" tri-metallic coinage operating in the central provinces of the Mughal empire – all except the copper paisa with a distinctly Islamic appearance.

Under Akbar this currency system became the foundation of the land revenue settlement and the entire structure of remunerative entitlements and rewards, as well as "ranks," of the official bureaucratic and military institutions. By being precisely computed in money values, these could acquire a greater degree of systematization than the far less monetized institutions of fiscal management and tributary flows in kind that had characterized the regimes of his predecessors. The highly developed currency system, with its ancillary monetary instruments such the *hundi* or "bill of exchange" and short-term credit, also facilitated the Mughal imperial nobility's investment of venture capital in industrial activities (such as, for instance, textile production in Bengal, or trade, and even shipping). In general, it was a great catalyst of economic development.

THE IMPERIAL POLITICAL SYSTEM AND ITS INDIAN FOUNDATIONS

The key to his success as an institution builder, however, is Akbar's creation of a new framework for his imperial service nobility – one that accommodated the leadership of the Hindu majority population in prominent positions and at the same time safeguarded its autonomy. This too was not new, either in theory or in practice. But Akbar made it official policy. In this way he set limits to the centralization of the empire, and in doing so put it on more secure foundations. The paradox is that Akbar's "dominion-increasing" policy succeeded because it was a policy of restraint.

The *mansab* or "ranking" system of the less than two thousand men who constituted the imperial nobility and were the "steel frame" of the Mughal Raj represented a single, unified hierarchy which did not exclude the Rajputs but rather (at least in the beginning) the Afghans as the representatives of the ancien regime. Mansabs were official "places," usually of combined civil and military power, which did not differentiate between Hindus and Muslims as such. They were perhaps the most striking aspect of the systematization which occurred under Akbar, in that they converted the rank, payment, and the military and other obligations of their holders (mansabdars) into exact numbers. The numbers – ranging from 10 to 10,000 – indicated the number of men that the mansabdars were expected to bring in. Akbar did not maintain a large standing army paid from the treasury but relied on such mansabdars to raise and command their own contingents of (mostly) cavalry. The ranks and attendant emoluments – which were obtained from centrally supervised *jagirs* or "assignments" of revenue collection in particular localities and which took up over 80 percent of the imperial budget – were not inheritable. Appointment, retention, promotion, and dismissal depended on the will of the emperor. The mansabdars were not an independently organized body and were not required to drill or observe uniformity in dress or arms. Here as everywhere, Akbar introduced regulations – including minutely descriptive rolls and the branding of horses – to ensure that the recruitment of the specified amounts of men, horses, provisions, and equipment took place. The jagirs or rights of revenue collection in particular localities were normally assigned for a few years only, and they involved merely the rights of revenue collection, not administrative, judicial, or residential rights (in contrast to what had often been the case with their medieval antecedents of *iqta's*). The higher mansabdars frequently held such land revenue assignments, large and small, in a number of non-contiguous villages and districts.

While it is possible to trace the basic notion of decimal military ranks to Chingis Khan, the actual vocabulary of the mansab system appears to have been introduced by the Indo-Afghan ruler Ibrahim Lodi (r. 1517–1526), not Babur or Humayun. Ibrahim Lodi employed an early form of the mansab system among his nobility in an attempt to undermine the Afghan custom of patrimonial sharing of revenue rights among clan members and did not incorporate the Rajputs in it. Akbar, in the eighteenth year of his reign (1573), gave the system the comprehensive and systematic features that it would retain during the remainder of the sixteenth century and throughout the seventeenth, except that the numbers were corrected for inflation (by multiplying the ranks) at the beginning of the reigns of both Jahangir and Shah Jahan.

When Akbar came to the throne, the major part of the country was under the rule of numerous, mostly small but at times substantial, hereditary "rajas" or "kings." As a group these were referred to by the Indo-Muslim imperial overlords as *zamindars* or "landholders." Akbar continued his predecessors' policy of demanding recognition of his "paramountcy" through the payment of tribute and the provision of military service from these potentates. In return the latter would enjoy autonomy in the internal administration of their realms, various forms of outside support, and the renewal of their hereditary titles. The prestigious Rajput houses of Rajasthan – the most powerful and pedigreed of this category – and perhaps a few hundred others became linked to the Mughal family through matrimonial ties. Akbar forged matrimonial relationships with their women, thereby ensuring that future Mughal emperors would have Indian "blue" blood, while the Rajput princes themselves, in their turn, would have a stake in the prosperity of the future Mughal dynasty. Akbar's son and successor Jahangir was born of one such marriage and was therefore half Indian. Shah Jahan married no Indian wives, but he was three-quarters Indian himself – since both his mother and grandmother were Rajput princesses. Some twenty rajas are said to have been in constant personal attendance at Akbar's court at its height. Many more were represented at either the imperial or the provincial courts by relatives or agents. Most significantly, however, many of these rajas, and some other influential Indians (like the Hindu finance minister Todar Mal), were absorbed into the imperial hierarchy of the mansabdars, receiving lucrative and honorable employment, as well as jagirs the revenue of which far exceeded that of their hereditary dominions. According to the calculations of Muhammad Athar Ali, in 1595 Rajputs held four of the 25 "highest mansabs" of 3000 and above; Rajputs, other Hindus, and Indian Muslims held 32 of the 98 "high mansabs" of 500 to 2500, and 47 of 160 "medium mansabs" of 200 to 450. The proportions were not very different half a century after Akbar's death. In 1656 Rajputs and Marathas held four of the 25 "highest mansabs" of 5000 and above; Rajputs, other Hindus, Marathas, and Indian Muslims held 79 of 223 "high mansabs" of 1000 to 4500, and 82 of 270 "medium mansabs" of 500 to 900 (Athar Ali, xx). All hereditary dominions of the rajas were treated as *watan jagirs* or "hereditary jagirs," and even though the rajas frequently rebelled against imperial demands and regulations there is no doubt that Akbar was much more successful than his predecessors in making them partners in the imperial enterprise. In effect, the growth and development of these kingdoms or chiefdoms into real states was a direct function of the Mughal policy of indirect rule. The institutions of rulership and clientele in Rajasthan in particular developed greatly during the sixteenth and seventeenth centuries at the expense of kinship as a basis of organization. The Mughal government assumed the right to appoint successors to positions of rulership in Rajasthan, and in turn supported them with arms and resources in the form of *watan jagirs* inside Rajasthan and other assignments outside. With such added support the local rulers could consolidate their own spheres of authority and centralize their administrations. Relationships based on kinship and customary access by birthright were replaced by relationships based on service and monetary exchange. This process also included the increasing bureaucratization of these relationships as administrative procedures became more and more modeled upon those of the Mughal administration itself.

In all the other territories – under direct imperial rule – the Mughal administration encountered another category of zamindars, a rural gentry of "landholders" with old and vested rights which had historically arisen out of the agrarian function of colonization and settlement (which had a military dimension as well) but without rights of sovereignty like those of the rajas. They represented the mostly Hindu rural leadership, a rural class standing just above the peasantry.

Virtually all the directly ruled territories of the Mughals, comprising the bulk of the fertile plains of Hindustan, whether given out as *jagirs* or reserved as *khalsa*, i.e. "crown lands," were under their customary jurisdiction. Ensconced in mud forts with local crack troops, possessing detailed knowledge of and participating in rural society, these zamindars, of varying ill-defined powers, were indispensable in the preparation of the revenue assessment, the realization of the land revenue, and the efforts to maintain and extend cultivation. They played a vital role in the political, economic, and cultural life of Indian rural society, and on that level exercised tremendous power.

Since their hereditary rights preceded the advent of the Mughals, there was always a clash of interests between the government and both categories of zamindars, whether more or less autonomous native states of the first type or rural gentry of the second type. In practice, most of the administrative problems the Mughal emperor faced had to do with the recalcitrance of the zamindars. While it granted the rajas a curtailed autonomy in internal administrative affairs, in the directly ruled territories the Mughal government attempted to reduce the rural gentry as much as possible to the position of "intermediaries" between itself and the peasants. But since the zamindars represented rural society, their interests were always narrowly localist and parochial, and they were therefore hard to control. "It is the general custom of the zamindars of Hindustan," wrote Abu-l-Fazl, "to leave wrongfully the path of single-mindedness and to have an eye to every side and to join anyone who is triumphant or stirring up sedition" (AN, II, 96). Localized zamindar revolts were endemic throughout the Mughal dominions for much of the time, in spite of the fact that they had no chance of "liberating" their territories from Mughal rule and might be brutally suppressed. Well over two hundred such uprisings are recorded in Akbar's reign alone. Unrecorded outbreaks must have been innumerable. In actual fact, Akbar's subjects were continually in revolt against him.

Nevertheless, Akbar succeeded in putting Mughal rule on a firm fiscal basis because he could secure the long-term collaboration of the zamindars. If they were not enrolled as mansabdars, like the Rajput princes, they always received the kinds of support from the Mughal government – financial, military, political – which allowed them to stay on top of their own numerous local rivals. In the cultural sphere, close links between the zamindars and the imperial government contributed to the emergence of a cultural synthesis of Indian and Islamic traditions, rural and urban, which had been unknown in medieval times or at best had been an incipient characteristic of the regional kingdoms.

If, in the directly administered territories, it was the Mughal government's aim to reduce the entire Indian rural gentry to mere "intermediaries" or "officeholders," it attempted to do the same with the tribal populations – pastoralists, forest people, and the like –

which occupied large parts of the empire which were not under cultivation or very marginally so. The *Ain-i-Akbari* represents the tribal lands as properly measured and regularly assessed territories, not different from agricultural lands, and the term *zamindars* is used for tribal chiefs as well.

As "intermediaries," zamindars were officially entitled to 10 percent of the land revenue as compensation for their services to the emperor; the rest went by right to him. Historians have been able to calculate that in practice more than half of the land revenue stayed in the hands of the zamindari leadership – although the *Ain-i-Akbari* is notoriously self-contradictory and unreliable here. The picture of these rural magnates as "officeholders" was never accurate. An eighteenth-century Maratha treatise on government, the *Ajnapatra*, argues on good grounds that the zamindars may be called "officeholders" but that this is only a term of convention for they are in fact "the sharers of the kingdom."[4] The treatise explains that the zamindars are never satisfied with what they have and they have no intention of being loyal to the sovereign but rather aim to increase their power by encroachment on each other's lands and stir up sedition. Between the sixteenth and eighteenth centuries the power of the zamindars, in effect, did increase a great deal, and eventually it was they who brought down the Mughal empire by igniting coordinated revolts. It was at that time that the Indo-Muslim condominium which was the foundation of Akbar's empire and the reason for its success came undone. In simple terms, the Mughal empire in the end succumbed to its own success.

LAND REVENUE AND THE PEASANTRY

It comes as no surprise that the *Ain-i-Akbari* provides a jumble of information on the affairs of the imperial household: treasures, mints, coins, seals; the kitchen, perfumes, and the wardrobe; the arsenal and elephant stables; regulations for branding horses, for oiling the emperor's camels and injecting oil into their nostrils; the daily allowances of food for mules; the harem; the manner in which His Majesty spends his time; regulations for admission to court and etiquette; the muster of men; the prices of building materials, the weight of different kinds of wood; the divisions of the army, the mansabdars, and the infantry; the manner in which salaries are paid, or the food allowed to leopards; and a whole lot more. What does come as a surprise is the amount of detailed information it gives on the fiscal affairs of the peasantry. Medieval Indian sources have nothing of the kind. The peasantry constituted about 85 percent of the 110 million or so people that lived in Mughal India by the end of Akbar's reign (of a total Indian population of perhaps 150 million). In a part of the *Ain-i-Akbari* which is called "the statistical and geographical survey of the empire" we find a laborious compilation of provincial revenue offices; chapters on the classification of lands and the proportionate dues of sovereignty; nineteen years' rates (from 1560) for various crops ("carrots," "lettuce," "onions," "barley," and many other crops are specified) for the provinces (subas) of Agra, Allahabad, Awadh, Delhi, Lahore, Multan, and Malwa; the ten years' fixed settlement and the rates charged for various crops in Allahabad; an "account of the twelve provinces (subas)" of 1594; and the collection figures of numerous districts (sarkars) expressed in copper coins and measurements of the total number of *bighas* of each.

There is another body of evidence – corroborating the above – which confirms beyond doubt that Akbar collected a fabulous amount of revenue from the Indian peasantry. In effect, the collection of land revenue by the state was the dominant factor in the redistribution of wealth in the country. The proverbial amount – reiterated by the *Ain-i-Akbari* – was 40 percent of the total production or virtually the whole of the movable surplus. But there has been considerable conjecture about what exactly this figure represents, what the real "take" of the Mughal government might have been, and how it was collected. An analysis of the statistics in the *Ain-i-Akbari* of the total amounts of revenue actually remitted in combination with estimates of the population yields an average annual per-capita payment of less than one rupee per head of the population. Multiplied by 110 million this amounts to a great amount of money, but, going by the prices of the *Ain-i-Akbari*, it was no more than the equivalent of the value of one tenth of one acre when average cultivation per head was 1.08 acres. This weight may have become even less in the period after the 1590s.

The Mughal bureaucracy which collected the land revenue – whatever the exact amount – was ramshackle at best, under Akbar and in later times. Surveys once made would not be updated for years until it was discovered by chance that the real wealth of a district was twice that of the survey. There were enormous disparities between adjacent districts for no apparent reasons. Large parts of the empire, including the whole of Bengal, were never properly surveyed at all.

In Akbar's reign, as early as 1565 or 1566 Muzaffar Khan Turbati undertook measures against the financial confusion but of these we have no details. Two or three years later a new finance minister, Shihab Khan, tried to check the almost universal practices of embezzlement but still we get no details. Abu-l-Fazl merely says "he abolished the yearly settlement, which was a cause of great expense and led to embezzlements, and he established a rate, while his acuteness suppressed the fraudulent" (AN, II, 488). In 1570 Muzaffar Khan Turbati, with the assistance of Todar Mal, prepared a revised assessment of the land revenue based on estimates made by local revenue officials. Lowering the earlier assessment rates, which had been based on rough guesses, it reduced the discrepancy between estimated and actual receipts.

In the wake of the conquest of parts of Gujarat, in 1574 Todar Mal for the first time introduced systematic measurement as a preliminary to a "settlement" or "assessment" of the land revenue which would last for ten years. Again the revenue demand is described as lower than that of previous kings, but exact figures cannot be obtained. Payment could be in kind, but preference was given to money collections "at the market price."

In 1575 Akbar decided to divide the empire as it then existed, with the exception of Bengal, Bihar, and Gujarat, into 182 purely artificial revenue units each yielding one "krore" or ten million tankas, the equivalent of 250,000 rupees, each to be placed under an officer called a "karori." The experiment was not successful and was abandoned. The most important reforms in the fiscal administration were effected in the years 1579–1580, the twenty-fourth and twenty-fifth regnal years. Mughal India was then divided into twelve provinces, each with a governor (sipahsalar) and a full set of officials. The twelve *subas* comprised more than 100 *sarkars* or "districts" which themselves were aggregates of "parganas" (also called "mahals"). The statistics of the *Ain-i-Akbari* are arranged according to these divisions, without reference to the "krore" system. Abu-l-Fazl explains how the revenue was fixed in 1580:

> One of the events [of this year] was the fixing of the revenue for ten years. Inasmuch as time produces, season after season, a new foundation for rates, and there are great increases and decreases, there was a regulation that every year some experienced and honest man should send in details of the rates from all parts of the country. Every year a general ordinance was framed with respect to the payment of dues. When the imperial domains became extensive . . . these reports arrived late and at different times . . . There were losses and disturbances . . . There were excessive demands . . . and corruption occurred . . . A new system of payment of dues was introduced. The gist of the new system was that the condition of every pargana during ten years [apparently from the fifteenth to the twenty-fourth year of Akbar's reign] was ascertained, according to the degree of cultivation and the price of produce . . . The carrying out of this settlement was entrusted to Raja Todar Mal and Khwaja Shah Mansur.
>
> [AN, III, 412–414]

It seems that some of the essential features of this settlement of northern India were anticipated in Todar Mal's settlement of Gujarat. Accurate statistics for the first five years of this period not being available, the authority of "persons of probity" was accepted. Akbar and his advisers fixed the units of measurement (Akbar's *Ilahi gaz*, on which the size area of his *bigha* depends) as a necessary pre-liminary for the survey. The first step of the survey was measurement;

next came the classification of lands (based on the continuity or dis-continuity of cultivation); then the fixing of rates. The crops being numerous, Abu-l-Fazl's compilation of rates in tables is extraordinary but it is doubtful whether or not laborious analysis of them can yield results of value. Abu-l-Fazl himself was not a revenue expert and probably did not thoroughly understand the statistics he collected. British-Indian revenue authorities always displayed considerable skepticism about his statistical figures. The historical chronicles of the time tell us hardly anything about the working of revenue legislation in actual practice, except that constant revisions were called for and the remission of cesses. In 1585, the failure of previous administrative reforms is noted: "The accountants have not rendered clear state-ments, and have not observed the sacred regulations . . . They have based this business – which rests upon inquiry and investigation – on conjecture and approximations" (AN, III, 687–693).

Nevertheless, there is a clearly articulated memory in India of the standard measurement surveys which were executed in the directly ruled Mughal territories of Hindustan by Todar Mal in the late six-teenth century and, modeled on these, by the Nizam Shahi regent Malik Ambar, the Mughal diwan Murshid Quli Khan, and the Maratha king Shivaji in the Deccan in the seventeenth century. They had in common that, after defining the king's share as a proportion of the total proceeds, they converted this proportion into fixed and invariable rates of assessment per uniformly measured unit of land of each quality. After measuring and classifying the cultivated land Todar Mal assessed it per bigha according to a uniform standard for each class. This standard assessment, in Akbar's time, penetrated into a part of Khandesh and of Gujarat, but not to Bengal.

Whether, in the wake of these reforms, the condition of the peas-antry improved or worsened under Mughal rule and whether it was better or worse than in British India we do not know. Scholars have argued all of these positions, generally without being able to convince anyone.

Akbar, of course, is portrayed by Abu-l-Fazl as a steadfast friend of the peasantry. As such he introduced a new calendar, the "Tarikh-i-Ilahi"

or "Divine Era," which took effect at the beginning of the Persian
New Year and was entirely (even in respect of the great festivals)
based on solar months and years. Unlike the Hindu lunar system of
time reckoning, it did not make the months begin from the period of
advancing darkness but from that of advancing light (around
the eleventh of March). It was intended to obliterate the bewildering
diversity of regional calendars that prevailed in his time in India,
and more particularly to set aside the Hijra era which Akbar
thought unjust to the peasantry of his realm, or so he said: thirty-one
lunar years equaled thirty solar ones, so if the agricultural revenue
was collected on the basis of lunar years, whereas the agricultural
cycle depended entirely on the solar calendar, the peasants
would eventually pay taxes on agricultural income they had not
actually had.

Abu-l-Fazl, followed by other historians, portrays Akbar not only
as a friend of the peasantry but as a king with cosmic powers: "The
heavens revolve at his wish" (AN, III, 886); he was a "rainmaker" (AN,
III, 148, 876, 924, 1061) and "rain-stopper" (AN, III, 1060; TA, II,
510); he could cure illness "with his Messiah-like breath" (AN, III,
298) and make pestilential air wholesome (Ain, II, 132). The same
author also assures us that for as long as he ruled his reign was an auspicious time of "good deeds:" "the abolition of enslavement of
women and children in war" (AN, II, 224, 246–247); "the manumis-
sion of thousands of slaves" (AN, III, 558); the foundation of "poor-
houses" (AN, III, 381; MT, II, 277); "kitchens for the poor and hungry
in every city" (TA, II, 519; AN, III, 1063–1064, 1087); and "comfort
inns, with kitchens, for travelers" (AN, III, 136). But what was the
real condition of the masses?

The Italian historian Piero Camporesi has argued that what characterized the life of the masses in early modern Europe was, above
all, hunger and the recurrent famines or food shortages (Camporesi,
1989). Precarious and inadequate diets, generating protein and vita-
min deficiencies, reduced immunity against infectious diseases,
while impure water and food mixtures, food poisoning, the constant
nightmare of worms and choleric diarrhea, combined with living

conditions in humid and badly ventilated "hovels," and parasites everywhere, conspired to keep most people in an almost perpetual state of deprivation so haunting that it gave them hallucinations. Was it different in India under Akbar? Probably not. In India, agriculture, and the life of the peasantry, has always been a gamble on the monsoon. Its regular failings guaranteed that innumerable peasants, already "very miserable" (in the words of Athanasius Nikitin, a Russian traveler of the fifteenth century), suffered starvation and death during droughts and the accompanying widespread famines or moved to the brink of extinction at least several times in their lives. In medieval times drought-famines were among the most common catastrophes affecting the peasants as well as the townspeople in most parts of India. In Indo-Persian chronicles, drought and starvation are covered by the same word, *qaht*. But although drought, often lasting more than one or even two years, was the most common cause of famine, it was not the only one. All places in India, including Delhi, that bore the brunt of Timur's invasion of 1398 were affected by famine and epidemics in its aftermath. The great famine and epidemic (cholera outbreaks due to contaminated water, as well as malaria, typically outran starvation) which devastated vast areas of Hindustan and Iran in 1033 was probably less due to drought than to the effects of several decades of Turkish invasions which preceded it.

If Akbar's reign were evaluated according to the prevalence of both weather-related and man-made famines or food-shortages it would not look better than most of the reigns that preceded or followed it, and probably worse than some. During Akbar's reign, we see no improvement over time. We have incontrovertible evidence in several, independent sources that Akbar's reign virtually began and ended with widespread and prolonged famine so severe that it led not only to widespread death but also, in many places, to cannibalism, when all regular food resources and even the animal carcasses and hides had run out. In the first year of the Divine Era, a famine began, caused by a preceding drought, which apparently lasted for two years and was accompanied by a dreadful plague and dispersion of the population. Abu-l-Fazl mentioned this in the *Akbarnama*: "[In the first year of the Divine Era] there was great scarcity in the cities and villages of India, and there was a terrible famine in many parts, and especially in the province of Delhi . . . Men took to eating one another" (AN, II, 57). But Abu-l-Fazl had no hesitation in blaming this less than auspicious event on Akbar's predecessors: "Apparently it was the pain of the past coming out in evidence so that the blessings of the holy accession to the throne of the Caliphate, the inequalities of the time, and the crookedness of the world might all at once be removed" (AN, II, 57). Abu-l-Fazl revisited the same famine in the *Ain-i-Akbari,* providing more detail: "The capital was devastated and nothing remained but a few houses. In addition to this and other immeasurable disasters, a plague became epidemical. This calamity and the destruction of life extended throughout most of the cities of Hindustan. The distress of the times ruined many families and multitudes died" (Ain, III, 489). Akbar's chief propagandist noted only in passing that in later years there were recurrent problems with the food supply. Astrologers, he wrote, had predicted that in 1577 in some of the inhabited parts of India grain would be dear, "and so it came to pass" (AN, III, 316). Again, in 1596 there was a deficiency of rain, and high prices "threw a world into distress" (AN, III, 1063). Abu-l-Fazl did report the occurrence of a great flood, possibly a tsunami, in 1584, the twenty-ninth year of the Divine Era, at three o'clock one afternoon, that swept over an entire district on the coast, apparently in Bengal, for four and a half hours, killing nearly 200,000 "living creatures" (Ain, II, 135–136).

Abu-l-Fazl does not mention one very serious drought-induced famine which is recorded elsewhere near the end of Akbar's reign, in 1596, as having raged continuously for three or four years throughout the whole of Hindustan, accompanied by plague, depopulating whole cities, and leading to cannibalism (ED, VI, 193).

Other famines, combined with the unavoidable epidemics, are on record during Akbar's reign that were entirely or to an aggravated extent "the spoils of battle." The incessant movement of Mughal armies from 1572 onward that was to put an end to the existence of the independent Sultanate of Gujarat caused "a severe pestilence and a great famine" that raged during the last six months of the nineteenth year of the Divine Era, 1574–1575. Three historians other than Abu-l-Fazl describe it – two of them in considerable detail – and none of them mentions drought even as a contributing factor (TA, II, 457; MT, 189; TAK, 232–233). According to al-Qandahari:

> During the same year plague and famine visited Gujarat. The rulers considered these the spoils of battle, caused by filth and rotten stench . . . The pestilence continued for five or six months. People had not witnessed such awful disaster for a long time, they felt utterly helpless and dreadful. Many people left the province and became exiles. The intensity of pestilence was such that every day a hundred cart-loads of dead bodies were taken out of Ahmadabad, which were thrown into ponds and covered with mud. Those were in addition to the dead who were carried on biers and bedsteads and were properly buried. Commodities became so dear that men had to be content with a single loaf of bread per day . . . Graves could not be dug for burials . . . Ultimately the deadly pestilence spread over the districts of Pattan, Baroach, Baroda and indeed engulfed the whole of Gujarat . . . Provision for horses and camels was nowhere to be had. So they scraped the bark of trees, crushed it and made it soft by soaking it in water and fed their cattle on it. Its aftereffects were numerous.
>
> [TAK, 232–233]

Similarly, in Bengal, the relentless Mughal drive to clear the province of Afghan opposition that spanned Akbar's long reign appears to have been accompanied in 1575 by an outbreak of plague, particularly severe at Gaur, that if not caused was at least aggravated by the intemperance of the army in an otherwise unwholesome climate (AN, III, 226; ED, IV, 512). The consequences were described by Abu-l-Fazl in his usual florid prose: "Although in that year there was a strong wind of destruction in all the eastern provinces, which shook the pillars of life, in that city [Gaur] it amounted to a typhoon" (AN, III, 226). And, finally, in one other well-documented instance, in Kashmir, according to various sources (including Jesuit accounts), in the spring of 1597 there was a very severe famine, caused by the deficiency of rain but aggravated by the presence of Akbar's army. Abu-l-Fazl wrote: "Although by the coming of the victorious army the scarcity was increased, yet the Shahanshah's graciousness provided a remedy" (AN, III, 1087). Here again, Abu-l-Fazl deftly turns a calamity which was at least partly due to the disruptions caused by Akbar's imperial army on campaign into an opportunity for the emperor to perform "good deeds," in this case famine relief.

7

SERENE CITY OF UNIVERSAL TOLERANCE

An anecdote related by virtually all contemporary Mughal historians has it that some time in 1566 Akbar became annoyed that he could not play horse polo at night and began to think of something to do about it, with the result that he invented the burning polo ball. Made of palas wood, it gave off sparks when hit hard enough.

Some time in 1582, according to another anecdote, Akbar set out to disprove a mulla's theory that speech was a divine gift and not something acquired by practice. He bought some new-born infants from their mothers and locked them in a sound-proof building for three or four years. In this "dumb house" they were kept under guard with no one to speak to them. Akbar was right: the infants all turned out dumb, if they did not die.

These anecdotes are evidence that, the poor scholastic record of his childhood notwithstanding, Akbar had an inquisitive and scientific mind. In itself this was not uncommon in the Mughal dynasty. But what makes Akbar stand out is that he was constantly looking for ways to make new knowledge useful. In the half-century of his reign he transformed Hindustan by what we may call "applied science."

Akbar's grandfather Babur had regarded Hindustan as "a country of few charms" – it was excessively hot and lacked cool water, ice, running water in gardens and residences, grapes and musk-melons, carpets, good camels, horses, and dogs. Akbar set out to remedy these deficiencies one by one. At his initiative saltpeter came to be extensively used as a cooling agent, and we are told that the nobles were supplied with ice from the northern mountains and enabled to enjoy it the whole year around, while even some of the common people enjoyed it in the summer. Air conditioning became widely available in trellised chambers built from khas, an odoriferous grass (Andropogon Muricatum) on which water was sprinkled to produce the desired effect. Skilled agriculturists were ordered to sow melons and to plant vines from Turkistan and Persia, just as they were ordered to bring saffron cultivation from Kashmir to Begram, near Kabul. Cherries and apricot trees began to be cultivated for the first time. Other fruits, not locally procurable, began to be imported in abundance from distant regions. Akbar patronized the manufacture of woolen and silken carpets. He invented new designs of pashmina (cloth made of the finest wool), silk-cloth, brocade, rugs, and carpets. Camels were produced which were not inferior to those of Iraq, while quality horses began to be bred in Kashmir. Akbar made contributions to shipbuilding techniques (making it easier for ships to be launched by having them built on huge floating platforms). Remarkably for an illiterate emperor, Akbar taught people the use of a new type of (East India?) ink that could not be obliterated in water.

Akbar also displayed a strong interest in geography, world politics, and history. With his Jesuit visitors he poured over atlases to learn about the relative locations of Portugal and his own kingdom, discussed the death of King Sebastian of Portugal at Alcazar Kibir while fighting against the Muslims in 1578, and contemplated sending ambassadors to Cathay to find out who was the new ruler of that country in 1597. He had a large library.

> Among books of renown, there are few that are not read in His Majesty's assembly hall; and there are no historical facts of the past ages, or curiosities of science, or interesting points of philosophy, with which His Majesty, a leader of impartial sages, is unacquainted. He does not get tired of hearing a book again, but listens to the reading of it with more interest . . . Several works of history are continually read

out to His Majesty. Philologists are constantly engaged in translating Hindi, Greek, Arabic, and Persian books into other languages.

[Ain, I, p. 110]

AKBAR AND ISLAM

Badauni maintained that "rationalism" was one of the manifestations of Akbar's ignorance that prevented him from being a good Muslim and ultimately made him turn his back on Islam. Some time around the middle of his reign, he says, "Akbar had the history of Islam read out to him . . . [And] soon after, the observance of the five prayers, and the fasts, and the belief in everything connected with the Prophet, were put down as vain superstitions, and man's reason, not tradition, was acknowledged as the only basis of religion" (MT, II, 215). In the thirty-second or thirty-third year Akbar ordered people to give up the Arabic sciences (the exegesis of the Koran and the Tradition) and study only the "really useful ones" such as astronomy, mathematics, medicine, history, poetry, and philosophy (MT, II, 375).

Badauni does not go into the question why the emperor did not move into this "rationalist" direction until he was well into middle age. We can speculate, however, that it is probably no coincidence that Akbar's public turning away from Islam coincided in time with the elimination of his half-brother Mirza Muhammad Hakim as a potentially dangerous focus of Islamic orthodox revolt.

Up to around that time, Akbar is described as quite a staunch supporter of Sunni Islam. When he ascended the throne, according to al-Qandahari, he was "the emperor of faith . . . whose qualities resembled those of the Prophet Muhammad" (TAK, 43). The deposition of Bairam Khan was generally proclaimed a victory of Sunni over Shi'a Islam. In the seventh year of the reign, the first embassy arriving from Shah Tahmasp of Persia carried a letter describing Akbar as the "unsurpassed adherent of God's word and extirpator of polytheists" (AN, II, 264). The conquest of the fortress of Chitor was proclaimed by Akbar himself as the victory of Islam over infidels. A

fathnama or "declaration of victory" issued on March 9, 1568, con-
veying the news of this conquest to the officials of the Panjab, is full of
professions of intolerance and couched in the most aggressive language of Islamic orthodoxy. "As directed by the word of God," Akbar
announced in this document, "we, as far as it is within our power,
remain busy in jihad and owing to the kindness of the superior Lord,
who is the promoter of our victories, we have succeeded in occupying
a number of forts and towns belonging to the infidels and have established Islam there. With the help of our bloodthirsty sword we have
erased the signs of infidelity from their minds and have destroyed
temples in those places and also all over Hindustan" (Khan, note 16).

An edict (*farman*) from Akbar of the same period directs officials
to prevent the Hindus of Bilgram from practicing idol-worship and
to take steps to eradicate heresy from this district. When al-
Qandahari refers to the conquest of the fortress of Kamal Mir in
1578, he claims that Akbar was motivated by nothing except the
desire of raising aloft "the banner of Islam" and uprooting the foundations of unbelief. In 1578, the year in which Akbar laid the foundations of the Friday mosque at Fatehpur Sikri, he had the title "Amir
al-Mu'minin" ("Commander of the Faithful"), along with other titles
of a religious nature, added to his name in the Friday prayers in the
mosques throughout his empire.

In 1578 even Badauni still had sufficient confidence in the Islamic
faith of the emperor to present him with a valuable pocket Koran,
and a notebook with rare sermons by Hafiz Muhammad Amin, a
famous preacher of Qandahar. Badauni hints that the emperor was
saying the five daily prayers at the mandatory hours around that time.
The historian Nizam ad-Din confirms that in the years 1578 and
1579 Akbar still joined in the public prayers five times a day. Abu-l-
Fazl also leaves no doubt that in 1579 Akbar was still showing great
respect for the family of the Prophet Muhammad by raising numerous Sayyids – alleged descendants of the Prophet – to high offices and
dignities, even though he also regretted that Akbar at that time was
already taxed with Shi'ite convictions, which in the view of many
Sunni Muslims amounted to a form of apostasy. The last eyewitness

account of Akbar publicly performing the Muslim prayers dates from the early 1580s and comes from Monserrate. The latter saw Akbar performing his prayers "after the Musulman fashion" at the mosque of Ahalis (at the entrance of the Khyber Pass) on his way back from Kabul (Monserrate, 155).

Between 1576 and 1582, Akbar sent money to the Hijaz and supported the hajj. Throughout that period an Amir-i-Hajj or "Commander of the Pilgrimage" was selected from among the nobles at the court and dispatched under military escort with as much as five or six hundred thousand rupees and some ten thousand khilats or "robes of honor" to be disbursed in the Hijaz – among the needy natives and foreign pilgrims in that country as well as among the Sayyids and religious notables there. Money was also sent for the construction and repair of religious buildings. In the same period, Akbar supported the efforts of some of the ladies of the imperial harem, including Babur's sister Gulbadan Begam, to make the pilgrimage to Mecca. Indeed, he issued a general order that anyone making the pilgrimage was to be reimbursed from the treasury. As a result the number of pilgrims from India in this period of Akbar's reign was higher than ever before. He expressed an inclination to go to the Hijaz himself in 1576, but abandoned the idea under pressure from his court officials. In the next year, to general praise, he followed the Amir-i-Hajj for a few paces as if he were a pilgrim, with bared hands and feet, having shorn his head a little, and wearing the pilgrim's garb. Soon after he began raising objections to the way "greedy men at the shrines" embezzled his donations which were meant for the poor. The flow of rupees began to peter out. In a letter to the Sharifs of Mecca written in February–March 1582 Akbar excuses himself for not having sent the customary donations in the previous year by pointing out that he had been away in the Panjab and Kabul. In the same document he explains that, out of large-heartedness, he had decided to forgive his half-brother Mirza Muhammad Hakim his insubordination and to reinstate him in Kabul, on condition that he would revive the Sharia and strive for the amelioration of the lives of the Muslims in his realm.

Until the elimination of Mirza Muhammad Hakim, too, Akbar's habitual lifestyle of "traveling and hunting" (*sair-o-shikar*) typically included frequent short pilgrimages of *ziyarat* (visits to the tombs of Muslim saints) in India itself. He continued making these short pilgrimages in the years between 1562 and 1585, even when they started to provoke scorn in clerical circles by about 1579, if not earlier. To some degree, the Sunnis of India had always frowned on this practice, rejecting the claim of Sufi hagiographers that a number of such short pilgrimages to the tombs of saints was morally equivalent to one pilgrimage to Mecca. In Mughal India countless tombs and shrines were venerated by Muslims, and commonly by Hindus as well. Manucci somewhat contemptuously comments that "the Mughals have an easy method of devotion, consisting in visits to tombs great or small, in order to obtain what they are in need of" (Manucci, II, 13). By far the most important shrines were those of the three great historical founders of the first specifically Indian Sufi order, that of the Chishtis – Mu'in ad-Din (d. 1236) at Ajmer, Nizam ad-Din Auliya (d. 1325) at Delhi, and Shaykh Farid Shakarganj ("Baba Farid," d. 1266) at Pakpattan. These shaykhs were all buried in Indian soil after failing to make the pilgrimage to Mecca themselves. Their shrines drew Muslim visitors, including kings, from as early as the fourteenth century. In India the cult of dead saints and the circumambulation of their tombs, accompanied by sometimes lavish donations, were in practice popular substitutes for the great pilgrimage for all those who could not bring themselves to go to Mecca. Badauni wrote that Akbar was "extremely devoted" to Khwaja Mu'in ad-Din Chishti, the greatest of all Indian Muslim cult figures, who had established himself at Ajmer in the twelfth century, and whose *wilayat* or "spiritual dominion" extended all over India. Between 1562 and 1579 Akbar went there at least once a year, often part of the way on foot, sometimes accompanied by choice members of his harem, to obtain blessings for the most important military undertakings in his career, or to offer up thanks for his good fortune. It was the road traveled from Agra to Ajmer that Akbar upgraded with madrasas, sarais, wells – and stags' horns. If he stopped traveling this road after 1579, he still sent his son Prince Daniel to Ajmer in 1581. He himself continued to visit other shrines throughout this period, some until as late as 1585; these included, among others, the "shrines of Delhi," and the shrines of Shaykh Farid Shakarganj at Pakpattan, in the Panjab, and that of Shaykh Jamal at Hansi.

At the same time, from about as early as the second half of the 1570s, there is unmistakable evidence that the emperor was on a collision course with Islam. The trajectory of his apostasy is described in different ways by contemporary authors but none of them appears to have been in doubt about the nature of the outcome.

According to Monserrate, whose description pertains exclusively to the first few years of the decade of the 1580s and is partly driven by the hope that the emperor was on the brink of converting to Christianity, the king's kindness to the Jesuits gave currency to "the rumor" that he had abjured Islam. Already at the time of the Jesuits' arrival at the court of Agra, however, Akbar was "not in the habit of saying the customary Musulman prayers at the times appointed by Muhammad, and did not observe the month's fast which is called Ramadan." Monserrate added that Akbar had already then "enraged many Muslims," so much so that a conspiracy was brewing to depose him on religious grounds and install his brother "Mirsachimus" (Mirza Muhammad Hakim), who was king of Kabul and a "bigoted Musulman" (Monserrate, 63, 65, 67). The conspiracy unraveled when Akbar took action against him. But "Zelaldinus" (Akbar) remained an "infamous outlaw" in the eyes of the Muslims: he had openly declared that he was not a Muslim and attributed no value to the creed of Muhammad, but was rather a follower of a sect which called upon God alone. He had begun to regard Muhammad himself as "a wicked and impious villain" and could not bear his name to be invoked (Monserrate, 83, 177).

For another description we may turn to a Sunni Muslim whose career was ruined by the emperor, the historian Badauni. He first brings up Akbar's growing hostility to Islam in the context of the latter's resumption of Muslim charity lands, which caused hardship among the ulama, in the years following 1576. From then up to the closing year of his history in 1596, Islam only deteriorated further. Careless with dates, Badauni records that, after five or six years (after 1576?), "not a trace of Islam was left in him [Akbar] and everything was turned topsy turvy" (MT, II, 262). Akbar, according to him, had started to regard the Islamic religion and all its doctrines as a senseless invention of some poor Arab highway robbers in but recent times. And as a result Islam allegedly became practically moribund in Akbar's reign. It was all due, if not to his apotheosis of "reason," then to the pernicious influence of "Hindu wretches" and "Hinduizing Muslims" on the ignorant emperor's mind; and it was made worse by the fact that villainously irreligious ulama pronounced the emperor blameless even while he heaped unrestrained insults upon the Prophet. Soon after the revocation of the charity lands, in fact, renowned scholars of Islam had vanished from the cities of India; a new generation appeared which neglected prayer, and abandoned madrasas and mosques.

According to Badauni, not every mulla acquiesced; some issued responses (fatwas) on the duty of rebellion against the irreligious emperor, and engaged in desperate struggles. But Akbar made sure that such mullas, and anyone whom he even suspected of dissent, were banished to the remotest parts of the empire, such as Bhakkar in Sind and similar places in Bengal. Numerous mullas, shaykhs, Sufis and fakirs were also deported to Qandahar and there exchanged for Turkish colts. It was in this way that the ulama of Lahore were scattered, and that the great shaykhs of Jaunpur with their wives and families were sent to Ajmer, where they languished in poverty or died. The grandson of Khwaja Mu'in ad-Din himself was banished to Bhakkar when he failed to make his proper obeisance to Akbar after returning from Mecca, and with the approach of the end of the first millennium the emperor abandoned all remaining respect for shaykhs and ulama, annulling the statutes and ordinances of Islam.

The real outrage, however – Badauni repeats this again and again – was not that Akbar committed all these violations of the one true religion, but that so many were prepared to follow him. Apostasy was rife. Swine and dogs were no longer regarded as unclean animals, but rather kept in the harem and under the fortress. Going to see them had become a neo-pagan rite of great popularity. The prayers of Islam, the fast, and even the pilgrimage were prohibited, or at times only the Friday prayer was retained, or the public prayers and the chanting of the azan five times per day were abolished in the state hall. The vestigial Islamic festivals also fell into disuse, the Hijra era was scrapped, on copper and gold coins the era of the millennium was introduced, and reading and learning Arabic allegedly came to be regarded as a crime. Muslim law and the exegesis of the Koran and the Tradition and those who studied them were "disapproved of." Names like Ahmad, Muhammad, Mustafa, and so on became offensive to His Majesty. Mosques and prayer rooms were turned into storerooms and locker rooms. The cemetery within the walls of the city was allowed to run to waste. In the end, the cult of the emperor "sent beards flying."

Another enraged Indo-Muslim scholar and Sufi reformist of the time, Shaykh Ahmad Sirhindi (1564–1624), gives a similarly gloomy description of the condition of Islam in Akbar's India. He acknowledges that people's belief in prophecy was on the wane, as was their compliance with the Sharia. Akbar, to him, was "one of the tyrants of our age" who had tortured many ulama because of their strict compliance with the Sharia and their unflinching obedience to the prophets (Friedmann, 33). Sirhindi confirms that the situation was so bad that the name of Muhammad could not be mentioned at court. The tyrant prohibited the sacrifice of the cow, demolished mosques, and paid honor to pagan temples.

Abu-l-Fazl, on the other hand, displays an unmistakable ambivalence toward Akbar's changing religious attitudes. In the recordings of the twenty-fourth Divine Year from the Holy Accession (1579–1580) in the *Akbarnama* he writes: "A set of evil-thinking, shameless ones imagined that the Prince of Horizons regarded the Muslim religion with disfavor. The sole evidence which those wrong-headed ones, whose understanding was rusted, had for this was that the wise sovereign out of his tolerant disposition and general benevolence, and extensive overshadowing, received all classes of mankind with affection. Especially did he search for evidence in religious matters from the sages of every religion and ascetics of all faiths" (AN, III, 398). In the *Ain-i-Akbari*, however, Abu-l-Fazl has Akbar say: "Formerly I persecuted men into conformity with my faith and deemed it to be Islam. As I grew in knowledge, I was overwhelmed with shame. Not being a Muslim myself, it was unbecoming for me to force others to become such. What constancy is to be expected from proselytes by compulsion?" (Ain, III, 429). Abu-l-Fazl himself, at the end of his life, is reported to have regretted his own and Akbar's departure from Islam: "Had I possessed a lofty spirit," he confessed, "I should not have descended from the summit of the heights of unity to the level of polytheism; but what is to be done?" (Ain, III, 459). In short, Abu-l-Fazl too admits that Akbar apostatized, even though he denies it at the same time. This makes the testimony virtually unanimous.

THE RELIGION OF GOD

Even among contemporaries, there was a great deal of speculation about the reasons for Akbar's apostasy from Islam. Those hostile to him, like Badauni, often ascribed it to his "ignorance" and to the influence of the Hindus at his court, or to that of his Hindu wives. There can be little doubt that such an influence was exerted and played an overwhelming role. But we should not assume that Akbar, with his imperious personality and his natural inclination to take the lead in almost any situation, was a passive recipient in this process of religious transmission. Even less should we assume that he acted out of purely "political" considerations in an attempt to come to terms with the religious diversity in his "ever-expanding dominion" – although that too was one of the results of his religious repositioning and it may have influenced the timing of his public admission of it.

What we do know about Akbar is that he had on several occasions (fairly wide apart) a particular type of religious or mystical experiences (Persian *jadhba*) that profoundly changed his thinking about religious questions and the way he conducted his entire life. Akbar had these experiences, sometimes accompanied by fits, from at least the age of twenty (more likely sixteen) to at least thirty-four. They had nothing to do with politics. On the contrary, they typically occurred on occasions when Akbar was "not constrained by the presence of short-sighted men and became averse to the servants of fortune's threshold who always attended on his stirrup, and separated from them" to engage in "prayerful communion" with his God alone (AN, II, 92–93). The descriptions we have of these experiences, together with other passing observations of a psycho-historical nature, indicate that Akbar's religious predisposition is perhaps best characterized as a specific form of "melancholy," something akin to what in Turkish culture has long been known and validated as *hüzün* ("sadness") (cf. Pamuk, Chapter 10). The word conveys a feeling of deep spiritual loss, either from having invested too much in worldly pleasures and material gain, or in the Sufi sense of spiritual anguish that one cannot get sufficiently close to God, because one cannot do enough for God in this world. In this tradition of Sufi mysticism it is the absence, not the presence, of melancholy that is deplored.

Melancholy is explicitly attributed to Akbar by the Jesuit Pierre du Jarric, who also linked it to epilepsy.[5] Among the sayings of Akbar recorded in the *Ain-i-Akbari* is this description of it: "My mind is not at ease in this diversity of sects and creeds, and my heart is oppressed by this outward pomp and circumstance . . . On the completion of my twentieth year, I experienced an internal bitterness, and from the lack of spiritual provision for my last journey, my soul was seized with exceeding sorrow" (Ain, III, 433). Abu-l-Fazl refers to it in the *Akbarnama* as well, under the seventh year of the reign: "The world is in the contemplation of the Shahanshah's genius an extremely contemptible affair. He does not deem it worthy of his complete attention, and always keeps his soul attached to the importance of God" (AN, II, 277). This alone will have made Akbar uneasy with what we may call "official" religion and drawn him into the orbit of ascetics, saints, and divines of all possible sects. Akbar apparently came to embrace the melancholy of the Sufi mystic, and from there moved on to new — supracommunal, non-sectarian — forms of a higher religious understanding that dispensed with the prophets.

Badauni, unsurprisingly, put these matters rather differently. It seemed to him that Akbar, from childhood to manhood, and from manhood to his declining years as emperor, had always shown a peculiar talent for selection and thereby came to combine within himself various pieces from various religions and opposite sectarian beliefs. In Badauni's view there was, however, a relatively brief period in which Akbar was especially devoted to stimulating theological debate among the various sects, and this was crucial in the religious development of the emperor. That period was between 1575 and 1582. Around 1575 Akbar was beginning to feel more secure in his power and had, at last, the opportunity to come into closer contact with religious ascetics, more specifically with the disciples of the late Mu'in ad-Din Chishti of Ajmer, and to spend more time discussing religion with them. He would spend whole nights in religious discussion and worship, "and from a feeling of thankfulness for his past successes he would sit many a morning alone in prayer and meditation on a large flat stone of an old building which lay near the palace in a lonely spot, with his head over his chest, gathering the bliss of the early hours of dawn" (MT, II, 202). A year or so into this period, Akbar decided he needed a special building for theological seminars on a grander scale. This is what motivated him to repair the cell of a former Chishti Sufi, Shaykh Abdullah Niyazi Sirhindi, in Fatehpur Sikri, and to build a spacious hall around it, next to a tank, which, when it was completed by 1576, he called the 'Ibadatkhana or "House of Worship." Here Akbar resumed his theological disputations in a more formal setting until he was compelled to leave for Kabul to deal with his half-brother. Upon his return, he resumed the debates interrupted by war for a time, but conducted them in his own private apartments rather than in the House of Worship. Attendance at these sessions gradually dropped off and then came to an end when he introduced his "Din-i-Ilahi," the "Religion of God" or "Divine Faith," and had it officially approved by a council of scholars.

We have to recall that formal theological debates of the kind sponsored by Akbar, and the attitude of openness and receptiveness that was at the heart of it, were not a novel phenomenon in the Mongol world. The *Itinerarium* of William of Rubruck provides evidence that as early as the mid-thirteenth century the Mongol Khan Möngke held exactly such debates with local Nestorians, Muslims, and Buddhists, together with Rubruck himself as the Christian protagonist. Moreover, some Afghan leaders of Akbar's time held theological disputations on a regular basis – confining them, however, to Muslim scholars. Thus Sultan Sikandar Lodi summoned the mullas of his empire to regular theological meetings at Sambhal. Sulayman Kararani, the Afghan leader in Bengal – to whom Akbar was paying the closest attention – nightly offered up his prayers in the company of some hundred and fifty renowned shaykhs and ulama, and then would remain with them until the morning, listening to commentaries and exhortations before returning to the business of state. Akbar was more methodical and more thorough than any of these rulers; and, as usual, he was a lot bolder.

All contemporary historians of Akbar's reign, including Abu-l-Fazl, are in agreement with Badauni that the House of Worship was the crucible of the new-fangled Religion of God, even when they tell the story differently. At first, if we can rely on Badauni's account, there were meetings in the House of Worship once a week after the Friday prayers. Almost immediately ill-feeling arose among the shaykhs, theologians, and amirs invited to represent their diverse religious points of view about their order of precedence. Seating arrangements were then introduced, and quantities of perfume distributed, as well as large sums of money as rewards for merit and ability. The meetings soon became more frequent and began to be held on other days of the week as well, although the ones on Friday nights still tended to go on the longest. The antagonism between the disputants of various religions and sects became more intense. Accusations of "heresy" were rife, the very bases of religious belief undermined. Akbar was prone to become annoyed with the frenzied, often defensive and gladiatorial exchanges that went on under his patronage.

Badauni observed: "They cast the emperor, who was possessed of an excellent disposition, and an earnest searcher of truth, but very igno-rant, a mere novice, and used to the company of infidel and base per-sons, into perplexity, until doubt was heaped upon doubt, and he lost all definite aim, and the straight wall of the true Law was broken" (MT, II, 263). The emperor continued, however, to have private con-versations with "crowds of learned men from all nations, and sages of various religions and sects" coming to his court (MT, II, 263). According to Badauni, he selected whatever appealed to him from any of these sages but took nothing from the Muslims. Abu-l-Fazl in essence agreed, but proclaimed it, in his turn, the triumph of reason over bigotry: "The Shahanshah's court became the home of the inquirers of the seven climes, and the assemblage of the wise of every religion and sect . . . reason was exalted . . . and the bigoted ulama and lawyers of orthodoxy found their positions difficult to defend" (AN, III, 366). According to Abu-l-Fazl, Akbar invited Sufis, philosophers, orators, jurists, Sunnis, Shi'is, brahmans, Jains, Christians of various denominations, Jews, Zoroastrians, and still others to the "beautiful, detached building" of the House of Worship, and made a rigorous examination of the principles of all their faiths and creeds. The astute sovereign praised whatever was good in any of these faiths and creeds.

PEACE FOR ALL

What was new about the Religion of God was, above all, that it involved a massive recycling of the old. For strict Sunni Muslims like Badauni, Akbar was capitulating to the "endless and innumerable host of Hindu believers" (MT, II, 265), "trying to please the princesses in the harem" (MT, II, 319). In the House of Worship the infidel brah-mans introduced the emperor to the secrets and legends of the reli-gion of India, allegedly turning him into a passionate devotee of idols representing the chief gods of the infidels. According to Badauni, Akbar became especially firmly convinced of the truth of the doctrine of metempsychosis. He shaved off the hair on the crown of his head and let the hair at the sides grow, because he believed that the soul of perfect beings, at the time of death, passed out by the crown (the tenth opening of the human body), with a noise resembling thunder. The accursed Birbar, "Prince of Poets," a brahman musician and a confidant of old, persuaded the emperor that since the sun gives light to all, ripening all fruits and products of the earth and sustaining the life of mankind, it should be made an object of worship and veneration, together with fire, water, stones, trees, and all natural things, even cows and their dung. Akbar thus introduced the worship of the sun at the festivals celebrated at the beginning of each new Divine Year. He also began to mutter spells, which Hindus taught him, to subject the sun to his wishes. He ordered that the sun should be worshiped four times a day, in the morning and evening, and at noon and midnight, and had one-thousand-and-one Sanskrit names for the sun collected and read daily at noon, while he devoutly turned toward the new object of worship. Later, again in order to show respect for the sun, he ordered that coffins should be placed in the graveyard on the eastern side of the city, and the dead should be buried with their heads toward the east, as he himself would do to go to sleep too. Zoroastrians or "Parsis" came from Nousari, in Gujarat, and persuaded Akbar of the superiority of the religion of Zarathustra. He put Abu-l-Fazl in charge of the sacred fire, prostrated himself before the sun in public, and ordered the entire court to rise up respectfully when the lamps and candles were lighted. He prohibited the slaughter of cows, and the eating of their meat, while permitting the meat of wild boar and tiger. Associating with yogis, he limited the time he spent in the harem, curtailed his food and drink, and abstained from meat eating himself, encouraging others to do the same. Abolishing the jizya or "poll tax" on Hindus, he adopted the brahmanical thread, began wearing the Hindu mark on his forehead, and mandated the wearing of gold and silk dresses at prayer time. In miniatures accompanying the Persian translation of the Ramayana epic, prepared by Badauni at Akbar's court around this time, Akbar was projected as "King Rama" fighting "demons."

Shaykh Ahmad Sirhindi blamed the spread of infidel customs and the translation of the infidels' laws into Persian with the alleged aim of obliterating Islam on the remoteness of Akbar's time from the Prophetic period, as well as the study of the science of philosophy and the books of "Indian sages" (*hukama' al-hind*) (Friedmann, 34).

Many of the basic features of Akbar's new religion are confirmed by less blinkered observers than Badauni or Sirhindi. Monserrate, for instance, wrote: "At this time the King was showing greater and greater favor to the Hindus, at whose request he had forbidden the sale of buffalo-flesh in the meat-market . . . Furthermore he had caused a wooden building of ingenious workmanship to be constructed, and had it placed on the very highest point of the palace-roof: and from this he watched the dawn and worshiped the rising sun" (Monserrate, 184). Akbar, it was widely reported, betrayed a predilection for the "infidel customs" of India throughout his life, even in the early years when he was still regarded as a good Muslim. From his early youth he liked to associate with brahmans, musicians, and Hindus of all kinds, and displayed a fondness for Hindi terms. In compliment to his Hindu wives he had continued to offer the *hom*, the branch of a tree which was a substitute for Soma juice and played a role in their religious ritual. Akbar had the tax on Hindu pilgrims abolished as early as 1563. In 1566 he adopted the Hindu custom of having himself weighed against precious metals twice a year, disbursing the resulting sum among brahmans and others. Years before he built the House of Worship, he had occasionally marked his forehead like a Hindu, and had jeweled strings tied to his wrists by brahmans by way of blessing, a practice that was imitated by his nobles. It had already then become the custom to wear the *rakhshika*, the amulet formed out of twisted linen rags worn on the wrist. He always drank the sacred water of the Ganges, both at home and on his travels. It was brought to him in sealed jars, from the district of Sorun when he was in Agra or Fatehpur Sikri, and from Hardwar when he was in the Panjab. Akbar allowed separate judiciaries for Muslims and Hindus. He tolerated, even praised, the practice of sati, the immolation of

Hindu widows, even though he prohibited its imposition and allowed Hindu widows to be remarried.

His fondness for Europeans remained a subject of conversation in Mughal India throughout the seventeenth century. It was, to say the least, remarkable in a country where to some Muslims even to hear the name of Christian or Frank was hateful, and blue eyes were regarded as a sign of hostility to the Prophet. Akbar employed a great number of Europeans in his service, as lapidaries, enamellers, gold-smiths, surgeons, as well as gunners. Many of them were Catholics. They petitioned for their priests to be settled in Agra, and as early as 1575 Portuguese Padres were sent for from Goa. These were fre-quently questioned about their beliefs by the emperor himself. By around 1580 the rumor that Akbar had become a worshiper of the Virgin Mary, the Mother of God, had become so widespread that one of the nobles, without the king's knowledge, had a picture of her installed on a bracket in the wall of the royal balcony at the side of the audience-chamber where the king would show himself to the people. Badauni said that Akbar "firmly believed in the truth of the Christian religion" and that for this reason he ordered Prince Murad to be educated in Christianity, while charging Abu-l-Fazl with the translation of the Gospel (MT, II, 262). Monserrate wrote that the Jesuit fathers were "inexpressibly eager" to reach the king's court, as they were confident he would embrace Christianity. In the sublime assemblies in the House of Worship, according to Abu-l-Fazl, "Christian philosophers assailed the orthodox (mutaffiqan)" (AN, III, 398). Akbar professed to believe in the stories of Christ's miracles and had pictures of Christ, Mary, Moses, and Muhammad installed in his dining hall. He prostrated himself on the ground in adoration of Christ and his mother and told his sons to do the same. All three princes became very close to the Fathers and were taught Christianity out of a little book. With regard to his sons, Akbar declared himself to be following the example of his ancestor Chingis Khan, who had ten sons and allowed each of them freely to choose his own religion, one of them thus becoming a Christian. The Jesuits kept ready for many days a condensed instruction course, but then at the appointed time the king cancelled because he had decided to go hunting and wanted to sleep. When the appointment was rescheduled, Akbar slept straight through the meeting, having taken his opium drink again.

Inevitably Akbar was caught up in what came to be known as the Mahdi movement of the turn of the first Islamic millennium. The idea of a Mahdi or Restorer of the Millennium was revived, with Akbar's approval, during the discussions in the House of Worship at Fatehpur Sikri. But it was inverted. Akbar himself was identified as the Lord of the Age through whom faded Islam was to come to an end — not be revived. Abu-l-Fazl took part in the composition of a "History of the Millennium," in which Islam was represented as a thing of the past.

The historians of Akbar's reign recorded a millenarian jumble of titles used in documents issued by or on behalf of Akbar. It was characteristic of the new Religion of God that it at once established Akbar as the "Mahdi," as the "Just King" (Sultan-i-'Adil), the "Caliph of the Age," the "Mujtahid of the Age," and arguably, as will be seen, as God himself. The title of "Just King" (Sultan-i-'Adil) or "Just Imam" (Imam-i-'Adil), according to one such document mentioned by Badauni, was conferred by the principal ulama in 1579. While conferring the title of the "Just King," or the "King of Islam," and the "Shadow of God" on Akbar, the ulama at the same time acknowledged he was the highest religious authority in the country. The document, signed or sealed by the principal ulama and lawyers (against their will in some cases, according to Badauni), explicitly stated that, from the year 1579 onward, in religious questions Akbar's opinion would overrule the opinions of the Mujtahids, the highest religious dignitaries, throughout Hindustan — now the center of security, peace, justice, and benevolence. Akbar's orders would be binding for all, provided only that they would be in accordance with some verse of the Koran and of real benefit. The same document is mentioned by Abu-l-Fazl, who wrote that it established the spiritual primacy of the emperor as the "Imam of the Age" and the "Mujtahid of the Age." The year 1579 was the year in which the emperor was anxious to unite in his person both the temporal and the spiritual authority of his dominion – he had heard that the Prophet, some of the Caliphs, and some powerful kings such as Timur had also led the Friday prayers themselves – and most of all to establish himself as the "Mujtahid of the Age." He did indeed mount the pulpit. But when he began to recite the Friday prayer in the chief mosque of Fatehpur Sikri, he stammered and trembled, and quickly came down from the pulpit, handing over the duties to a court reader.

The mahzar or decree of 1579 – sometimes called Akbar's "Infallibility Decree" – has been a subject of controversy ever since it was issued. It has been argued, on good grounds, that it aimed not merely at establishing Akbar's spiritual supremacy but also at rejecting the nominal overlordship of the Shi'a Safawid emperors of Iran, which Babur and Humayun had been forced to accept as a condition for Safawid military support in the conquest of Hindustan. In this regard it may be significant that the Mughal historians applied the title "Caliph of God" or "Caliph of the Age" to Akbar – as well as to his successors, by endowing the Sufi term "Caliph" with what were regarded as its full Sunni connotations. From then on, Sunni Islam in Mughal India stood for independence from Persia, while Shi'ism stood for Persian suzerainty. It also meant that the Mughal capital became the "Home of the Caliphate" and this in turn induced the emperors to assume a leading role in the prayers, as we see at times throughout Mughal history from Akbar onward. But in 1579, when Akbar determined publicly to use the sentence "There is no God but God, and Akbar is his Caliph" it caused commotion, and the objection was raised that it would enrage the Sultan of Constantinople. Akbar then decided to restrict the use of this sentence to the palace.

ALLAHU AKBAR

In the years between 1579 and 1585 religious and secular bureaucracies expanded in parallel. The Religion of God helped consolidate a more intensive form of state supervision and control, and the expanding bureaucracies provided the means to implement changes — simultaneously fiscal, political, social, and religious — which had the potential to reach every subject.

New marriage regulations were introduced to foster a new ideal of the healthy family. It was forbidden to marry one's cousin or near relation because in such cases the sexual appetite was but small. Boys were not to marry before the age of sixteen, girls not before fourteen, because the offspring of such marriages was weak.

The Religion of God also became the "source of confidence and promotion" (MT, II, 314). During this same time four degrees of devotion to the emperor were defined, depending on one's readiness to sacrifice one's property, life, honor, and religion. In a word, promotion came to depend on abject surrender to the emperor. For Akbar it was but a short step from "spiritual primacy" to apotheosis. If in India no one had ever set himself up as a prophet, he reasoned, it was because claims to divinity had superseded it.

Akbar's own claim to divine status hinged on the interpretation of the formulaic phrase "Allahu Akbar," with its ambiguity of meaning. It could, after all, be translated both as "God is Great" and as "God is Akbar." The emperor first proposed to have this phrase carved on his seal, and on the dies of his coins, as early as 1575 but desisted in response to Muslim objections. Now he allowed it to become a mark of the highest of the four degrees of devotion to him. Among fourth-degree "devotees" ("chelas," a technical term for "disciples" among yogis) it became the established routine to have one's writings prefaced by "Allahu Akbar." These devotees were beardless men who greeted each other with the words "Allahu Akbar" instead of "Salam," who flung themselves on the floor before the emperor, and who wore his likeness in a jeweled case on top of their turbans. There could be no mistaking the white-hot loyalty, the standard of sincere friendship, or even the happiness, in this "vanguard of righteousness."

Outside the palace, a crowd of emperor worshipers from among those who were not admitted into its precincts would gather every morning, opposite the window at which Akbar would pray to the sun. Here too rose the cry "Allahu Akbar" when the emperor appeared on view. Every evening there was another crowd, now of needy Hindus and Muslims, men and women, healthy and sick, "a queer gathering and a most terrible crowd" that prostrated itself no sooner than Akbar had finished reciting the one-thousand-and-one names of the Great Luminary and stepped on to the balcony (MT, II, 335). "Cheating and thieving brahmans" told the emperor he was an incarnation of Rama and Krishna, and produced Sanskrit verses from ancient sages who had predicted that a great conqueror who would honor both brahmans and cows would arise in India and cover the earth with a carpet of justice. They wrote these Sanskrit verses on old-looking paper and showed them to the emperor, who pretended to believe every word of them.

What Akbar meant to bring about was fulfillment of a dream of universal tolerance. The great new religion that it was his deepest desire to advance, as he made clear almost from the beginning of his reign, consisted of "binding the multitudes of the inhabited world on the thread of unity" (AN, II, 246). His only desire was "that every class of mankind may become religious and worship God in accordance with the measure of their faith" (AN, II, 205). In 1587 it was proclaimed, again in the words of Abu-l-Fazl: "The world lord exercises world sway on the principle of 'universal peace,' every sect can assert its doctrine without apprehension, and everyone can worship God after his own fashion" (AN, III, 804). In the words of Badauni: "No man should be interfered with on account of his religion, and anyone was allowed to go over to any religion he pleased" (MT, II, 405). And in Akbar's own words: "It is my duty to be in good understanding with all men. If they walk in the way of God's will, interference with them would be in itself reprehensible; and if otherwise, they are under the malady of ignorance and deserve my compassion" (AN, III, 430). Jahangir recalled this about his father: "He associated with the good of every race and creed and persuasion, and was gracious to all in accordance with their condition and understanding . . . This was different from the practice in other realms, for in Persia there was room for Shi'is only, and in Turkey, India and Turan there was room for Sunnis only" (Tuzuk, I, 37–38). The outspoken Jesuit Monserrate, however, unable to hide his disappointment, commented bitterly: "He cared little that in allowing every one to follow his own religion he was in reality violating all religions" (Monserrate, 142).

AFTER AKBAR: THE DEMISE OF THE RELIGION OF GOD

For Akbar, India in the sixteenth century was a raucous, intoxicating, and, above all, crowded bazaar of religious ideas, convictions, divine revelations and commands, as much as delusions. To the extent that his new political theology of the Religion of God advocated – even enjoined – the universal tolerance of all religions and sects that were on offer in this bazaar it could and did keep at bay murderous conflicts of the sort that rocked Reformation Europe. Divine revelation did not *need* to result in murderous politics. But universal tolerance was not every Muslim's dream, just Akbar's.

In the century after Akbar's death, the Mughal court went through something like an Islamic revival. The Religion of God with its bizarre manifestations of "discipleship" and emperor apotheosis, and much of the theatrics attendant upon it, had never spread much beyond the court and faded out slowly under Akbar's immediate successors. Jahangir still had an eclectic interest in the spiritual unity of all religions and continued some of his father's religious practices in the earlier part of his reign. But almost immediately the imperial attitude to Islam became stricter. Afterwards, the Islamic cast of the Mughal government gradually became ever more pronounced.

Both Jahangir and Shah Jahan regarded themselves, at least in theory, as Muslim kings and upholders of the Muslim law. They renewed links with the powerful Sufi orders of the Chishtis and Naqshbandis, visiting and endowing their shrines. Shah Jahan strove to distance himself from his father by assuming a much more traditional attitude toward Islam, at least in public, even while still a prince. He undertook concerted attempts to make policies conform to the Sharia, proscribing prostration before the emperor, and curtailing the construction of new Hindu and Jain temples.

Aurangzeb favored a strict adherence to Sunni Islam, amplifying Shah Jahan's increasingly Islamic policies. Modern historians (from Jadunath Sarkar onward) have often compared him unfavorably with Akbar. They hold Aurangzeb responsible for the reversal of Akbar's policies of tolerance, suggesting that he promoted an aggressively Islamic state that discriminated against Hindus and other non-Muslims, contributing thereby, in the early eighteenth century, to the decline of the empire. Aurangzeb's policies also came to be seen as foreshadowing more murderous politics. The communalist conflict which shaped South Asia's modern history is alleged to have originated with his reversal of Akbar's legacy of tolerance. His Hinduizing brother Dara Shikoh (1615–1659), by contrast, has generally been seen as the true heir of Akbar in the seventeenth century – coming close to apostasy himself. But Dara Shikoh became an early victim of the more murderous politics, justified by religion, initiated by his ruthless brother Aurangzeb.

Aurangzeb's personal Islamic piety is undisputed. He brought about further changes in court ceremony, suspended the jharoka-i-darshan or "public viewing" of the emperor, and prohibited music at his court. He commissioned the *Fatawa-i Jahangiri*, a multivolume text written in Arabic and subsequently translated into Persian, which was a compilation of Hanafi legal decisions. He re-introduced the jiziya or "poll tax" on non-Muslims from 1679 onward.

It is, however, significant that the secular toleration of Hindus and other non-Muslims remained the cornerstone of imperial Mughal rule up to the very end. The diversity of the Mughal ruling class was always maintained. In the last decades of Aurangzeb's reign the percentage of Hindus in Mughal service in fact reached a new height. Rather than the Religion of God, this secular and pragmatic alignment of Hindus and Muslims in the empire was perhaps the most important part of Akbar's legacy.

8

BEING AKBAR

Leaving behind Akbar's "Body Politic," in this final chapter we now turn to his "Body Natural." The biographical data we can cull from written and visual sources is realistic enough to bring Akbar into focus as a historical person. It highlights important features of his appearance, his character and personality — even his temper. It also reveals important data about Akbar's personal life.

The minutiae of appearance befitted a king who had orchestrated his own apotheosis as the Indo-Muslim emperor of the sixteenth century. Portraits and miniatures of his time invariably show Akbar without a beard, but with a moustache like that of a Mongol youth who had not quite grown up yet. Historical sources confirm that Akbar shaved every day, or, more likely, had himself shaven by a Hindu barber every day. This "look" was apparently unknown to his grandfather Babur and his father Humayun, both of whom are invariably depicted with beards (in Babur's case we have no contemporary portraits, however). Akbar passed it on to his son Jahangir. Shah Jahan abandoned it at some point in his life. And Aurangzeb again always wore a beard.

A beard is what a Muslim male would normally have. The absence or length of the beard sent a powerful political message that was understood by everyone and, inevitably, carried instant religious connotations. Akbar shaved off his beard because the Rajputs did so, his intention being to win them over. By 1582, it had become a mark of special devotion to him.

Akbar did not cut his hair short, nor did he wear a hat, but rather gathered up his hair in a turban, with long protruding whiskers. This was contrary to the general Mongol custom. It was also un-Islamic, and another concession to the Rajputs and his other Indian subjects.

Other than that, Akbar looked like a Mongol. His eyelashes were very long; his eyebrows black although not strongly marked. His face was ordinary, lean and wrinkled, of no special grandeur, becoming almost distorted when he laughed, but with a broad and open forehead. His complexion was not very fair, rather dark, but light brown, the hue of wheat. His nose was straight and small, his nostrils wide. Between the left nostril and the upper lip there was a fleshy mole, the size of half a pea, which was considered very pleasing in appearance and a sign of exceedingly good fortune. His eyes were black and small, extremely vivid, and bright like sunlight. "When he looks at you," wrote Monserrate, "it seems as if they hurt you with their brightness, and thus nothing escapes his notice, be it a person or something trivial, and they also reveal sharpness of mind and keenness of intellect" (Monserrate, 36–37). Akbar cast his bright eyes around the room, sizing people up "with the dissimulation of a very prudent and wise man" (Letters, 74). By the standards of the time, he was of middle height, inclining to the tall, "tiger-shaped" (sherandam), with a broad chest and broad shoulders, large bandy legs well-suited for horsemanship, and long arms and hands. He had the body of a "divine athlete." He was well-built, neither too thin nor too stout, but sturdy, hearty, and robust. Physically fit and an avid sportsman, he was known for his extraordinary physical strength and valor.

His countenance, all sources agree, reflected his royal dignity, and identified him as the king at first glance. His expression was serene and open, also full of dignity, and of awe-inspiring majesty when he was angry. He carried his head bent toward his right shoulder, and, like Timur, limped with one of his legs, although he had never been injured there. His voice was very loud, and had a peculiar richness. According to his son Jahangir, "in his actions and movements he [Akbar] was not like the people of the world, and the glory of God manifested itself in him" (Tuzuk, I, 33).

By most accounts, Akbar dressed plainly. Out of indifference toward the things of this world, he wore woolen clothes, as the Sufis did, especially shawls. "Notwithstanding all his power he is a man who is very ordinary and simple in dress, food, and in the people he has at court," observed Father Acquaviva (Letters, 57). But the emperor is also described as contemptuous of Muhammad's clothing instructions in that he wore garments of silk, embroidered in gold. He was not uncommonly seen in robes, turbans, and breeches made of very fine white muslin, with shoes on his feet of embroidered scarlet wool which looked expensive. He wore gold ornaments, pearls, and other kinds of jewelry at all times. He even designed some of his own clothes, such as the military cloak which came down only as far as his knees, as was the Christian fashion, and his boots, which covered his ankles completely. Privately he sometimes wore the Spanish dress. Never without arms later in life, he was especially fond of carrying a European sword and dagger. While he generally sat, with crossed legs, on a couch covered with scarlet rugs, he also had a velvet throne made in the Portuguese fashion which he carried along with him on his journeys. He traveled, often in elaborate state, on "softly-going she-camels," on horseback, or in the hauda of elephants, not uncommonly by river boat, on foot only when on pilgrimage, in a litter only when ill or wounded, but at times he also went around in a bullock cart, and he had a two-horse chariot in which his appearance was very striking.

A man of great energy and enterprise, Akbar used to go about incognito, when young, to pry into people's minds, as Henry V of England would do in taverns and among soldiers on the battlefield. "There is nothing he does not know," says Father Acquaviva (Letters, 56). In matters of war he was pre-eminent, in matters of government very skilled, he understood and discussed all laws. And he delighted in any mechanical art, and often put his hand to them. He sometimes quarried stone himself, along with the workmen. Some considered Akbar slightly crazy because he was very dexterous at all jobs, making ribbons like a lace-maker, and filing, sawing, and working very hard. Fond of amusements, he preferred those of a martial kind: elephant fighting, buffalo fighting, stag fighting, cock fighting, boxing contests, battles of gladiators, next to horse polo and pigeon flying. He was also very fond of strange birds, and of any novel objects. He amused himself with singing, concerts, dances, conjurers' tricks, and jesters, too. For recreation he kept a variety of deer, panthers, cheetahs, elephants, fighting cocks, vultures, eagles, camels, dromedaries, and pigeons.

Akbar may have had three alcoholic sons, but that was not because he had driven them to alcoholism by being a cold-hearted or bad father. To the best of our knowledge he was fond of children and a family man with a warm personality. He was deeply grieved by the number of his children, male as well as female, who died within months, even though very high child mortality was a normal fact of life in sixteenth-century India, even in the Mughal family. And it is notable that he did not kill his half-brother Mirza Muhammad Hakim even when circumstances would have warranted it.

He enjoyed spending a good deal of time with the women kept in strict purda in his harem, and often took them along on his travels. He was especially devoted to his mother, Hamida Banu Begam (who was adamantly opposed to his Christian leanings). He always let his mother, sisters, and other ladies of the harem go first. When his aunt Gulbadan Begam returned from Mecca, he had the pavements covered with silken shawls, and escorted her personally to her palace in an ornamental litter, scattering largesse to the crowds.

Monserrate griped that Muslim potentates in general "employed the sanction and license of the foulest immorality in order to ratify peace and create friendly relationships with their vassal princes or neighboring monarchs. For they marry the daughters and sisters of such rulers" (Monserrate, 202). Akbar, according to Monserrate, had more than three hundred wives, for each of whom he reserved a separate suite of rooms in a very large palace. Abu-l-Fazl put the number at "more than five thousand," perhaps reflecting a situation twenty or more years after Monserrate, but in all likelihood exaggerating for propaganda purposes. "His Majesty forms matrimonial alliances with princes of Hindustan and of other countries," wrote Abu-l-Fazl, "and secures by these ties of harmony the peace of the world" (Ain, I, 45).

We can divide Akbar's "wives" into three classes: women that he married in a formal *nikah* ceremony for reasons that were not primarily political (limited to four in Islamic law, but in Akbar's case certainly exceeding that limit); free women that he took into his harem for reasons primarily political (not recognized as wives under Islamic law, and in practice unlimited in number); and concubines (unlimited in number under Islamic law and taken, in Akbar's time, from slaves of geographically and ethnically diverse backgrounds or – in violation of Islamic law – obtained from free women through *droit de seigneur*). The first class was the most exclusive by far as it was made up of the women that Akbar officially had children with – few in fact, only three sons and two daughters surviving by the early 1580s. The second class included many Indian women, but also the daughters of the old Muslim nobility of Delhi and Agra, and others to boot. Political liaisons were often seen as expedient by all parties but they were by no means always welcomed. Certainly in the beginning, when it was still entirely novel, Akbar's "marriage policy" sent shockwaves through Rajasthan. When in 1564 he sent his brokers (qawwals) and eunuchs into the harems of the Delhi nobility for the purpose of selecting some of their daughters, "a great terror fell upon the city" (MT, II, 59). The third class we must assume was primarily made up of women that Akbar at one time or another considered desirable. If he produced more children in this class, as seems probable (because other kings always did), we know next to nothing about them. A good number of these concubines may have been simply picked off the street. We are told that the most beautiful women in the realm belonged to the emperor by right. According to Badauni, if the emperor "cast his eye with desire on any woman" she could, according to the law of the Mughal emperors, simply be requisitioned, already married or not (MT, II, 59). And Manucci wrote about Akbar: "Since, also, there was in the world no other king of greater valor or of greater wealth than himself, therefore the most beautiful of women were his by right. If she were not delivered to him he would harry the whole kingdom with fire and sword in order to accomplish his desire" (Manucci, I, 122).

Above all, Akbar loved to be surrounded by, or at least keep within sight, large crowds of people. Images of Akbar often place him among crowds in action scenes, whereas Jahangir and Shah Jahan are frequently depicted alone in portraits. As Monserrate observed: "His court is always thronged with multitudes of men of every type, though especially with the nobles, whom he commands to come . . . When he goes outside the palace, he is surrounded and followed by these nobles and a strong body-guard. They have to go on foot until he gives them a nod to indicate that they may mount" (Monserrate, 198). Akbar is frequently described as extremely affable and accessible, and as generally displaying cheerfulness to his people. Even though he was easily excited to anger, he soon cooled down. As Father Henriques put it: "He being naturally gifted with every good sense and understanding . . . He is very simple and courteous toward everyone, and always cheerful, but with a great dignity such as one expects from a very great king" (Letters, 21–22). "And so he is very courteous and sensible, and extremely dignified, and is much feared by his subjects. To his people he displays a certain amount of cheerfulness which in no way detracts from his imperial bearing," wrote Monserrate (Letters, 37). By nature simple and straightforward, he was a man of excellent judgment, prudent and affable, and gentle even in his youth. As Jahangir remembered him, "no sign of vanity or snobbery ever appeared on his face . . . [and] notwithstanding his kingship and his treasures and his buried wealth, which were beyond the scope of counting and imagination, his fighting elephants and Arab horses, he never by a hair's breadth placed his foot beyond the base of humility before the throne of God, but considered himself the lowest of created beings" (Tuzuk, I, 37).

Affable or not, being an apostate was a high-risk position. For some Muslims it was an unforgivable offence, for which only the death penalty was appropriate, as that was the law. Monserrate recorded that when Akbar was beginning to be suspected of apostasy he started to go about armed at all times, fearing he would be assassinated (Monserrate, 197). In the light that assassination was always expected, it is, in effect, somewhat surprising how few serious attempts were made. The first, and somewhat faint, attempt was part of the conspiracy to put his half-brother Mirza Muhammad Hakim on the throne. On that occasion, in 1564, Akbar was hit by an arrow in the Delhi bazaar. The arrow struck his shoulder and penetrated fairly deeply. He lay ill for week, then recovered. This assassination attempt actually occurred long before his apostasy. But he remained on high alert ever after it. Dishes were brought into his dining hall covered and wrapped in linen cloths tied and sealed by his own cook, for fear of poison.

Akbar was wounded in the groin during a battle in Gujarat in 1574, and freak accidents also took their toll. He fell from his horse while pursuing a hyena in Daka, in Kashmir, and was badly wounded, hitting his head on the stones, in 1589. He was even more badly wounded and knocked insensible when he fell off a female elephant later in the same year, on his way back from Kabul – this time his condition was serious enough to trigger off sedition and plundering raids in places wide afar. In 1595 panic broke out throughout Hindustan when Akbar was gored in the testicles by an antelope. The horns penetrated frighteningly deep, and Akbar was in excruciating pain for twenty-nine days until he recovered.

Akbar's health record is incomplete. But we know that, like virtually everyone else, he went through a range of maladies throughout his life. Chickenpox in 1561, numerous ill-defined afflictions caused by the climate and excessively long marches, internal pains, stomach aches and colics, toothaches, constipation induced by the use of opium, and various bladder and urinary-tract conditions possibly set off by the use of aphrodisiacs, repeatedly inconvenienced the emperor in later years and by the end of his life gave rise to the suspicion that he was being poisoned by Prince Salim. Akbar fell terminally ill in 1605, the same year his son Daniel died, and a year after the death of his mother. He broke down very quickly then and died on October 15, 1605. As with so many kings (Herodotus knew at least seven accounts of Cyrus' death) there were many theories about his death. Most persistent perhaps was the theory — which was never proven, but is likely — that he was poisoned by Prince Salim, the future emperor Jahangir. Other rumors had it that he accidentally poisoned himself by taking one of the poison pills he held in reserve for his nobles in his betel-leaf box next to the throne.

Akbar had prepared a site for his mausoleum with great care. He had chosen a garden on the road to Delhi, at three leagues from Agra to the west, and named it – not so humbly – Sikandra, i.e. "Alexandria." It was Jahangir who erected a magnificent building here, with a very large dome, and a gilded and enameled roof, and with a large garden, allegedly paying 1,500,000 rupees for the whole edifice. For a long time there were drawings of human figures on it. In the principal gateway of the garden were a crucifix, the Virgin Mary, and St Ignatius – until Aurangzeb ordered a coat of whitewash to be applied over these. We don't know exactly what happened when Akbar's grave was vandalized by local villagers in 1691. The precious stones and all the gold work were reportedly all stolen. It is said that his bones were dug up and burnt in a fire. When Manucci visited the mausoleum near the end of the seventeenth century, everything appeared to be in perfect order again. In the beautiful, well-maintained garden, mullas were reading the Koran.

ENDNOTES

1. i.e. *musht* (Hindi for mad, sexually aroused). Elephants in this state are unusually aggressive and hence dangerous.
2. Mathew Paris, the St Albans historian, in the 1240s described the Tartars as "inhuman beings resembling beasts, who one should call monsters rather than men, who are thirsty for blood and drink it, who seek out and devour the flesh of dogs and even human flesh."
3. Chapter 3, p. 24; for more detail see also Chapter 6.
4. A. Wink, *Land and Sovereignty in India: Agrarian Society and Politics under the Eighteenth-Century Maratha Svarajya* (Cambridge, 1986), p. 186.
5. "Natura erat melancholicus, et epileptico subjectus morbo" (Pierre du Jarric, *Thesaurus Rerum Indicarum, II* (Cologne, 1615), p. 498).

FURTHER READING

Binyon, L., *Akbar* (New York, 1932).

Gascoigne, B., *The Great Moghuls* (London, 1971).

Habib, I., *Akbar and his India* (Delhi, 1989).

Malleson, G. B., *Akbar and the Rise of the Mughal Empire* (1891; reprint Delhi, 2005).

Richards, J. F., *The Mughal Empire* (Cambridge, 1993).

Smith, V. A., *Akbar the Great Mogul, 1542–1605* (Oxford, 1919).

BIBLIOGRAPHY

MUGHAL SOURCES

Ain

Blochmann, H. (transl.), *The A'in-i-Akbari*, 3 vols (Delhi, 1977); idem (ed.), *The A'in-i-Akbari of Abu-l-Fazl* (Bibliotheca Indica no. 58, Calcutta, 1867–1877).

AN

Beveridge, H. (transl.), *The Akbarnama of Abu-l-Fazl*, 3 vols (Delhi, 1979); Ahmad Ali, A. (ed.), *The Akbarnama*, 2 vols (Bibliotheca Indica no. 79, Calcutta, 1873–1887).

ED

Elliot, H. M. and Dowson, J. (eds), *The History of India as Told by its own Historians*, 8 vols (London, 1867–1877).

MT

Ranking, G. S. A. (transl.), *Muntakhabu-t-Tawarikh by Abdul-Qadiri ibn-i-Muluk Shah al-Badaoni*, 3 vols (Delhi, 1990); Ahmad Ali, M. (ed.), *Muntakhab at-Tawarikh*, 3 vols (Calcutta, 1864–1869).

TA

De, B. (ed. and transl.), *The Tabaqat-i-Akbari of Khwajah Nizamuddin Ahmad*, vol. II (Calcutta, 1996).

TAK

Ahmad, T. (transl.), *Tarikh-i-Akbari of M. Arif Qandahari* (Delhi, 1993); Azhar Ali Dihlawi, H. M. and Ali Arshi, I. (eds), *Tarikh-i-Akbari by Haji Muhammad 'Arif Qandahari* (Rampur, 1962).

Tuzuk

Rogers, A. (transl.), *Tuzuk-i-Jahangiri or Memoirs of Jahangir* (Delhi, 1989).

EUROPEAN SOURCES

Du Jarric, P., *Thesaurus Rerum Indicarum, II* (Cologne, 1615).

Letters

Correia-Afonso, J. (ed. and transl.), *Letters from the Mughal Court: the First Jesuit Mission to Akbar, 1580–1583* (Bombay, 1980).

Manucci

Irvine, W. (transl.), *Mogul India or Storia do Mogor by Niccolao Manucci*, 4 vols (Delhi, 2005).

Monserrate

Hoyland, J. S. (transl.), *The Commentary of Father Monserrate, S. J. on His Journey to the Court of Akbar* (Oxford, 1922).

SECONDARY WORKS

Athar Ali, M., *The Apparatus of Empire: Awards of Ranks, Offices and Titles to the Mughal Nobility, 1573–1658* (Delhi, 1985).

Bartold, V., *Sochineniia (Collected Works)*, vol. 6 (Moscow, 1966).

Barzun, J., *From Dawn to Decadence, 1500 to the Present: 500 Years of Western Cultural Life* (New York, 2001).

Camporesi, P., *Bread of Dreams: Food and Fantasy in Early Modern Europe* (Oxford, 1989).

Duffy, C., *Siege Warfare* (London, 1979).

Friedmann, Y., *Shaykh Ahmad Sirhindi: An Outline of His Thought and a Study of His Image in the Eyes of Posterity* (Delhi, 2000).

Gommans, J. J. L., *Mughal Warfare* (London, 2002).

Hardy, P., *The Muslims of British India* (Cambridge, 1972).

Hodgson, M. G. S., *The Venture of Islam*, 3 vols (Chicago, 1974).

Kaye, J. W., *A History of the Sepoy War in India, 1857–58*, vol. III (London, 1880).

Khan, I. A., "The Nobility under Akbar and the Development of His Religious Policy, 1560–80," *Journal of the Royal Asiatic Society of Great Britain and Ireland* (1968), pp. 29–39.

McNeill, W. H., *The Pursuit of Power* (Chicago, 1982).

Pamuk, O., *Istanbul: Memoirs of a City* (London, 2005).

Smith, V. A., *Akbar the Great Mogul, 1542–1605* (Oxford, 1919).

Streusand, D. E., *The Formation of the Mughal Empire* (Delhi, 1989).

Wink, A., *Land and Sovereignty in India: Agrarian Society and Politics under the Eighteenth-Century Maratha Svarajya* (Cambridge, 1986).

INDEX

Abdul Haqq, Shaykh 21
Abdullah Khan 37, 38, 39
Abu-l-Fazl 6, 25, 37, 47, 100, 102, 112;
    Ain -i-Akbari 5, 47, 53–4, 60, 62–3,
    64–5, 76–8, 79–80, 83, 96; *Akbarnama*
    5, 7, 9, 12, 18–19, 21, 30, 35, 37–43,
    45, 53, 55, 56–7, 61, 75, 78, 79, 80,
    83, 106; on famine 83, 84–5; on good
    deeds of Akbar 81; House of Worship
    99, 102; and Islam 89, 94–5
Acquavivia, Rudolfo 50, 111
Adham Khan 16, 20
administration, Akbar and 10, 52–3,
    64, 66
Afghans 16, 23, 30, 71; Mughal sense of
    superiority over 51; opposition to
    Akbar 18, 22, 34, 35, 41–2
Agra 17
agriculture 31, 87
Ain-i-Akbari see Abu-l-Fazl, *Ain-i-Akbari*
air conditioning 87
Akbar, Jalal ad-Din 1, 19, 36, 60, 64, 81;
    ancestors 2–3; appearance and dress of
    109–11; apostasy of 89, 92, 93–4,
    114–15; birth of 7; claim to divine
    status 105–6; cosmic powers 81;
    death of 115–16; degrees of devotion
    to the emperor 105; early life 8–9;
    education and training 10–14, 15;
    family of 112; as founder of Mughal
    empire 1–2, 64; grave of 50, 116;
    health of 115; as institution builder
    64–5, 66–76; military policy 24–6,
    27–8; opponents of 22–3, 32–4, 35;
    personality and characteristics of 14,
    63, 111–12, 114; and religion 95–103;
    scientific mind 86–7; titles of 16, 89,
    103–4; travels of 36, 37, 38–41, 43–4,
    91–2; wives of 16, 112–13
alcohol consumption 57–8; ban on
    drinking 58–9

'Allahu Akbar' 105–6
alliances 27–8, 73, 112, 113
Ambar Nazir, Khwaja 10
Amir-i-Hajj 90
amirs 24
artillery 26–7, 31, 66–8
asceticism 61, 96–7
Askari, Mirza (Akbar's uncle) 5, 8, 9
assassination attempts 114–15
Atak, fortress of 33
Aurangzeb (Akbar's great-grandson) 15,
    37, 48, 59,109; and Islam 108

Babur, Zahir ad-Din (Akbar's grandfather)
    2, 3, 27, 86, 109; gardens of 16; grave
    of 17; in Kabul 1, 17; rivals of 3–4
Badakhshan 9, 32, 33
Badauni 4, 49–50, 58, 91, 97, 106; on
    Akbar and Islam 88, 89, 92–4; on
    Christianity 102; on Religion of God
    98–9
Bahadur Khan 31, 41
Bairam Khan (regent) 8, 15, 19–20
Balkh 22, 32, 33, 34
Bartold, V. 66
beards 109
Bengal 22, 30, 34; conquest of 34–5;
    plague in 84
Bernier, F. 58
Bhimbar Pass 43
Bihar 22, 30, 34, 35
Birbar 100
Bukhara 2, 22, 46
bureaucracy 51–2, 65, 68, 70, 78, 104–5

calendar 16, 80–1
Camporesi, P. 81
carpet manufacture 87
cavalry 23–4, 24–5, 25–6, 68, 71
Chausa, battle of 6
cheetahs, hunting with 42, 55

121